John Sentamu's Faith Stories

John Sentamu's Faith Stories

20 True Stories of Faith Changing Lives Today

Presented by the Archbishop of York, Dr John Sentamu

Stories written by
Carmel Thomason

DARTON·LONGMAN + TODD

First published in 2013 by
Darton, Longman and Todd Ltd
1 Spencer Court
140 – 142 Wandsworth High Street
London SW18 4JJ

Reprinted 2013 (twice), 2014

ISBN: 978-0-232-52978-4

A catalogue record for this book is available from the British Library.

Phototypeset by Kerrypress Ltd, Luton, Beds.
Printed and bound by Bell & Bain, Glasgow.

Contents

Introduction

What is the point of the Christian faith in our modern world? Does it have any relevance in today's society?

During her Diamond Jubilee year, Her Majesty the Queen said: 'Faith plays a key role in the identity of many millions of people, providing not only a system of belief, but also a sense of belonging. Indeed, religious groups have a proud track record of helping those in the greatest need, including the sick, the elderly, the lonely and the disadvantaged. They remind us of the responsibilities we have beyond ourselves.' We need to hear and heed her wisdom.

One of the basic instructions God gives us in the Bible is to treat others as we would want to be treated ourselves. It is a 'golden rule' common to the world's religions. We need to be a voice for the voiceless and a champion for the marginalised.

We volunteer our selves – our gifts, our talents, our individuality – not because we feel we should give something back to those less fortunate than us, but because everyone is precious, of unique worth in God's sight and dearly loved by God. We have a duty and responsibility to those around us.

The Church of England knows all about volunteering. More people do unpaid work for church groups than any other organisation. Churchgoers contribute 23.2 million hours voluntary service each month in their local communities.

The church is involved on a daily basis trying to make the lives of people better. As one of my predecessors, Archbishop William Temple, said: 'The church is the only organisation that exists for the wellbeing and fraternity of its non-members.'

When we think of vocation, we tend to think of priests, or nurses and doctors, or teachers – but God is calling on all of us, on every single person, to fulfil our potential and use the gifts he has given us to serve others.

Each of us has an incredible story to tell. In this book I have collected a few examples of how individuals are putting God's vision of love and care into action in new and exciting ways. I hope these stories will inspire you as you travel on your own journey with the God who walks with us on the road of life.

We are not meant to hide away the good news of God and keep it to ourselves, we are meant to take our faith out into our communities and use it to make a difference. Let us encourage one another and offer support to those who are in need of God's love.

The church has been doing 'The Big Society' for over 2000 years – I hope these stories will help inspire us for the 2000 years that lie ahead for children yet unborn.

With God, the impossible becomes possible. The ordinary can achieve the extraordinary. Insurmountable barriers can be overcome, and those without hope become the inspirers. This is the greatest story ever told, and we are invited to participate in it.

Too often in life we can be discouraged by the size of the challenge before us. Instead of focusing on what we can do, we concentrate on what we can't do. The fact is, we can all make a difference.

When you look at a great cathedral like York Minster, it is easy to see that no individual could have created it singlehand-edly. From the imagining, to the planning, to the building – many hundreds of people helped to make the architects' vision a reality. Some laid the foundations, some built the walls and roof, others made the stained-glass windows or crafted the wonderful stone masonry. Working together, following the plans laid down in the beginning, a glorious glimpse of heaven was created within our city for the benefit of our nation. That is how we should see our small contributions in the lives of others. A small but important contribution to the greater good, allow-ing a glimpse of heaven on earth, benefiting the spiritual, moral and physical lives of the nation in practical ways.

With God, we are all called to serve and play our part in making our communities generous, safer and flourishing. True vocation is serving others and treating people as we would like to be treated ourselves.

If we all offered a small amount of time, talent and effort to improving life for those around us – just a little – together we could make a big impact on the difficulties we face as a country.

Cynicism is the disease of our modern age and the Christian virtue of hope is the cure. We need to believe, not only that a better future is possible, but also a better present too. We need practical outpourings of God's love, not good intentions and procrastination. As John Lennon once said: 'Life is what happens while you're busy making other plans.' So let's get out there and do something to make the world a better place!

God has the power to transform any and every situation. All we have to do is give ourselves to him and be ready to serve.

Why not take a risk? Live prophetically. In the words of Mahatma Gandhi: 'Be the change you want to see.'

Who knows, by your simple acts of selfless love and devotion you may inspire a radical change in our culture. You may already be leading the change within our nation without recognising it yourself.

Believe things can be better. Hope for more. Trust in God.

1   Keeping God at the Centre

Sarah Nicholson

Sarah Nicholson is a widow bringing up two young sons on her own in Cleveland. When her husband died suddenly, she started a blog, using writing to help her make sense of her grief. By sharing her experiences she came to accept that she couldn't rewrite her life, and discovered God could still surprise her in ways that she never imagined.

John Sentamu writes:

Life isn't always easy or straightforward. In fact there are so many ups and downs to be had that sometimes it feels like a rollercoaster!

Do you know the marriage vows that we say in church on our wedding day? They say we will take our husband or wife 'to have and to hold from this day forward, for better for worse, for richer for poorer, in sickness and in health, to love and to cherish, till death us do part'.

Those vows recognise that times will not always be good – but that we need to stand alongside each other in times of trial. I like to use an analogy that each marriage has three strands, the husband, the wife and God, each woven together making the relationship stronger and hopefully unbreakable.

And as the writer of the book of Ecclesiastes says, 'A threefold cord is not quickly broken' (Ecclesiastes 4:12).

Christians recognise that throughout all our personal upheaval God is a constant, present with us and helping us through.

And if we are parted from our spouse, what then? When everything is falling apart around us, we should remember that God is at the centre holding everything together.

This chapter looks at the story of Sarah, a widow who started writing a blog when her husband died suddenly at the age of forty-eight – a positive approach which helped her come to terms with her own grief, and has helped others experiencing bereavement.

✢

How do you mend a broken heart? I don't think anyone can really tell you that. For some questions there isn't an answer. Of course there are theories, lots of them. There are many models for grief too, all neatly written down in stages. By some reckoning I'm four down, so only one to go until I'm back to normal – as if.

I've learned that theory and practice are often two very different beasts. When it comes to it, you just have to move through grief as best you can, hoping that when you reach the other side you are in a better place to cheer on the next person who finds themselves hurting, encouraging them to carry on too. Does that sound like I've come up with yet another theory? I hope not. If I've learned anything, it is that there is no right or wrong way to deal with grief, and there certainly is no quick fix, no easy answers, and no magic pill. In the end we all have to find our own way – mine was writing.

Two weeks after my husband died I sat down at my computer and started a blog. Had things been different, we would have been celebrating Andrew's forty-ninth birthday. As it was, my life as I knew it was falling apart. We'd been married for sixteen years and had two boys, aged thirteen and ten. I was a stay-at-home mum, looking after the three men in my life. Now, my family was one less, and the hole Andrew left seemed to make everything unravel. Threads of my life were coming loose and I couldn't hold on to them, while others were being pulled so tight that they left me in physical pain. Whatever I did, and however much I tried, there was nothing I could do to stop it.

I thought that maybe writing would help. I called my blog *Unravelling Edges*, in the hope that writing it might help me begin to knit the threads of my life back together. It was partly for myself, to help me work through the many conflicting thoughts and feelings that were consuming me. At the same time I was always aware that by putting my words out there, on the internet, someone else might read them. I wanted to be heard. I knew that I might be churning out drivel, but I didn't apologise for that. Whatever I wrote was a genuine account of my life at that time and I wouldn't have shared it if I didn't want some company along the way.

Andrew's death in November 2010 was both sudden and shocking. We'd had a difficult start to the year. Problems at work had seen Andrew spiral down into another depression. It would hit him off and on throughout our marriage and he'd need to be alone, distancing himself, while the two boys and I were in another room, doing something together. Times like this were always very hard. However, by spring his work problems had resolved and even friends began to notice the old Andrew was back. He seemed more content with life, more generous and outgoing. I felt that we were together again in every sense, our relationship was getting better and better all the time – life was good. Then, one Saturday afternoon Andrew complained of a headache and went upstairs to lie down. I went out to visit a friend and told the boys that they needed to behave because dad was upstairs in bed. When I returned, a few hours later, the boys were still playing but the house seemed very quiet. I went upstairs to see Andrew and found him collapsed on the floor beside the bed. I shouted his name, but he didn't respond. Hearing me, my sons ran upstairs and my eldest helped me pull Andrew away from the bed. As he turned, I saw his face was blue. I dialled 999 and the woman at the other end told me to start doing cardiopulmonary resuscitation. I couldn't follow her instructions and hold the phone at the same time, so I repeated them out loud while our eldest son pressed hard on his dad's chest to try to get his heart pumping again. When the para-medics arrived I rang a friend to ask if she could look after the children while I went to the hospital with Andrew. It wasn't necessary. Andrew was already dead.

I never realised how much there was to do when someone dies – people to inform, papers and finances to organise, things to sort out, including a wardrobe of clothes that I knew would never be worn again. It was almost like I went onto autopilot, busying myself with all these things that needed to be done, until it snowed and I could do nothing.

In my mind the snow made what was already a bad situation ten times worse. It was hindering me, stopping me from doing all these extra things that suddenly needed to be done. I com-plained to a friend: 'I could cope with everything else better if it wasn't for the snow.'

'Maybe God doesn't want you to cope with it all,' she replied.

I thought about that. Without the snow I would have been running around like a mad woman, trying to prove that I could do it all. Yet here I was, forced by the weather to slow down, to take time and ask for help. Whatever I didn't get done would have to wait.

Later that afternoon I glanced out of the window. The set-ting winter sun had cast shadows of elongated bare trees, and watching its light reflected in the spaces between them on the ground sent a rush of excitement through me. Like a child I dashed downstairs, kicking off my slippers as I went so that I could run faster. I grabbed the camera from the kitchen, pushed

my feet into my wellies and ran out into the garden. The sight
was so beautiful I had to capture it. I wasn't sure that my photo
could do it any real justice, but I posted it on my blog to share.

Sometimes I felt guilty because I seemed to be getting on
with life. Andrew worked on an oil rig off the coast of Aber-
deen, so for most of our married life he'd be away from home for
weeks at a time. After he died I'd pretend that he was just
working away, trying to push reality to the back of my mind,
that this time he wasn't coming home. Other times I'd think
about when he was at home, but he was depressed and I felt
alone. Then I'd wonder, am I glad he's not here? Of course, I
wasn't, but I was different without him and things had
changed.

I didn't blame God for Andrew's death. I didn't think that God
caused it to happen, but I was angry with him. I knew that there
was hope somewhere, but I couldn't find it. I knew God was still
there, but I stopped talking to him. Soon, I stopped writing too.
This wasn't what my life was supposed to be. If I'd written the
story myself everything would be different. It felt like every
door I tried was closed. I didn't know what was happening. I
was trying to control things that couldn't be controlled, until
there was nothing to do but step back and let everything go.
That's when God surprised me.

Gradually I started writing again and people I had never met
began posting lovely comments on my blog. 'Oh, I'm so glad
you're writing again, your words have really helped me', wrote
one. In the back of mind I always held the thought that people
might read my words, that I'd like them to read my words, but
finding out that they did felt incredible. I couldn't quite believe
it. Someone had found what I had written, they'd read it and it
had touched them enough to contact me. To think when I was
broken and at my most vulnerable, God had used me to help
someone else – well, that just amazed me.

A year after Andrew's death I started another blog. This
time I called it *Re-ravelling*. I know it's not a real word, but what
is the opposite of unravelling? I don't know, but I thought if
Shakespeare can invent words then why can't I? Sometimes I'll

dip back into my old blog and it's nice to think that I'm not still in the same place. Other times I'll re-read it and think, aarrgghhh – I haven't moved. It can seem like I am going around and around in circles, but when I look closely, it's useful to be able to notice the small changes, where life is slightly different and where I still need to work. Life isn't about getting to one place and staying there. It's a journey and we're all a work in progress.

This summer I camped at New Wine, a big Christian conference in Newark. One morning I went into the shower and although there were two showers free, there was a queue.

'Are you waiting?' I asked.

The woman queuing replied, 'I'm not going in those two. I'm waiting for the other one – they're rubbish.'

The showers did have a reputation for being either a bit too hot or a bit too cold, and sometimes even non-existent. I stood for a while and then thought, we're camping, what does it matter? I don't need to wash my hair, a dribble of water and I'll be fine. I got into the shower and turned it on. It started with a bit of a dribble, then all of a sudden the water came out and it was a perfect shower. As the warmth filled my body, a huge grin spread across my face. I felt that God was saying to me – you are special and I love you. I have so much more for you than a dribbling shower, I've got so many blessings to pour on your life.

I think that sometimes we all live in the dribbling bits. For me, the past couple of years have been very tough. Life has often not gone as I've wanted it, no matter how hard I've tried to steer myself in a particular direction. At those times I'd get cross with God, behaving like a petulant teenager, who thinks that no one understands her. I recognise the same behaviour in my relationship with my own children. How they get cross with me sometimes, refusing to speak to me because I don't do exactly what they want. It doesn't mean that I love them any less or that I don't want the best for them. Of course, they can never see that at the time.

Children often believe that their parents haven't got a clue what's good for them, and I must admit that I'm guilty of thinking that about God too. Later, when I've calmed down and stopped trying to force everything to go my way, doors seem to open and God surprises me. Sometimes I feel his presence in the smallest of things, like that shower, and I'm reminded that even though life might not be going according to my plan, God has something else waiting for me, and it will be better than I think.

2   A True Vocation

Paul Birch

Paul Birch is Associate Director of Roughshod, which is the touring part of Riding Lights theatre company based in York. The company takes drama performances and workshops into prisons, schools, churches and other venues across the country, using stories to raise questions about lifestyle, values and the Christian faith.

John Sentamu writes:

Most of us like listening to a good story. Whether we are reading a book, watching a film or spending a night at the theatre, there are several ways to enjoy and engage with familiar words and images.

God's story, from the Earth's creation to the resurrection of Jesus from the dead, is the greatest story ever told. No one who has been to the York Mystery Plays, or to the passion play at Oberammergau, will ever forget the experience.

Each of us has our own part to play because this story is ongoing, developing all the time and branching out in new ways. We have a living story that is growing wider by the day and demanding to be heard.

As Christians, we all have our individual roles in the church bringing God's love to our wider society. You may feel that you can't achieve anything on your own, that your contribution is very small, but it is important to remember that we are not alone and with God anything is possible.

Think of a choir. As individuals we all have our bit to sing – on its own it may feel a tiny part, even fragmented and insignificant in isolation, but when you sing with the rest of the choir and all the parts come together, the harmonies and melodies create something much bigger.

God is our choir's conductor and he hears every unique voice and sees the wonderful contribution they make to the final song.

It is right that we celebrate our diversity, but we should also embrace what we have in common – an extraordinary God of love who is beyond our imaginings and at the centre of each of our unfolding stories.

This chapter looks at the story of Paul, someone who uses his gifts for story-telling to reach out in new ways.

When I was sixteen I thought that perhaps the best way I could live for God was to become a vicar. My vicar at the time told me: 'Where you've got gifts in certain areas, I think you should pursue those.' So I went to college and trained to be an actor.

Since then, I've never seen a separation between religious vocation and non-religious vocation. There are good places for each of us to be and that will be different for different people. A person who is a fantastic doctor, plumber or teacher is follow-ing his or her own vocation in life, just the same as someone who is called to be a missionary or a priest. A vocation may be for all of your life, or it may just be for part of it. There are different seasons and God uses us in different ways. I think that if you are a committed Christian your values will be reflected in whatever work you do.

I've always been passionate about drama and telling stories. Stories are powerful, in whatever form they happen, whether they are told in conversation, in a book, a film, a theatre production, a radio play, or even a YouTube video. Watching a situation played out in front of us can bring emotions to the surface, emotions that we may have hidden or ignored for some time. It can challenge views by offering a different perspective and help people to change the way they look at the world. To have a person act out a story in front of you has an extra power to it. That is why I chose to work in theatre. I love film, TV and radio, but for me, when theatre is good, it is the most powerful medium of all. Once someone is in that space, their attention is focused, it takes a lot to get up and walk out.

I've always found something very special about being in a room where a live performance is happening. It's not just about me or about one person's experience, there is a collective response that can be felt in the room. For example, if a play provokes a lot of anger or sadness, you will feel that emotion generated in the room, much more so than if that audience was watching in a cinema. There is something about the performers being in front of you that brings down barriers and makes the story feel all the more real.

When I was at university I had an intense spiritual experience while praying. I've shared my story in workshops; it raises a lot of different issues and some people have opened up about having similar experiences. At the time, I felt that it was God's way of saying to me, I am real and you can't just make up your own faith. You can't define your own lot and choose which parts of the gospel you want to follow and leave out the bits that you don't like. I changed my life from that point and made a full commitment to live for Christ.

I must have always had a sense of wanting to make a difference through my work, because when, after graduation, most of my class went to London in search of an agent, I decided to create a one-man show about environmental and social justice issues. For a year I lived by faith, touring up and down the country anywhere people would have me. I performed for free at universities, in churches, at festivals and conferences, even in people's living rooms. I realise now that it was a very rough show with many flaws, but something in it seemed to speak to people, it sparked discussion and I could see it was changing some people's views.

Seeing how theatre could be used to change hearts in this way was inspiring, but after twelve months of touring alone I felt that I needed to be acting with other people again. I heard about Riding Lights. The ethos of the theatre company spoke to me. It was exciting and innovative, taking theatre into places like prisons, to people who otherwise wouldn't get the opportunity to experience live performance. It promoted new writing too, told stories with a spiritual heart, and, although grassroots, was reaching about 65,000 people every year.

Working for Riding Lights seemed ideal to me, but when I rang the office I found out that the deadline for auditions had passed and I was too late to apply for that year. I was gutted, but just in case there was any chance at all I sent in a copy of my CV. Shortly after that I was invited for an interview. That was in 1997. I started working for the company and since then I've written, performed or directed at least one project for them every year.

You'll often see Riding Lights referred to in the media as a Christian theatre company. I don't like to use that term to describe the work that I do, because it doesn't really mean anything. It's impossible to have 'Christian theatre', because a Christian is just a person in relationship with God and theatre can't be in relationship with God, just as you can have a Christian painter, but you can't have a 'Christian painting', because a painting can't be in relationship with God. It is also unhelpful to describe us that way because some people bring a lot of baggage to anything they label as Christian. By that, I don't just mean people being suspicious of it. Even within the church, people hiring a Christian theatre company might expect a play or a piece of work to be a certain thing and that's not necessarily the case. It doesn't mean that we don't put on performances that advocate the gospel, but at the same time that's not the only type of show that we do. It is really important for us that we're not a ghettoised artistic community who panders to what people might expect us to do. As a company we hire Christians and non-Christians depending on what the project is and we do a lot of co-productions with secular organisations. We like being in relationship with people, whoever they may be.

I believe that God can use any work of art for good – it doesn't have to be created by a Christian or be prophetic to make a difference. A secular writer can write a play about Jesus that's not necessarily Christian and a Christian writer can write a play about a boy who loses his bicycle and that can be Christian.

I'm not sure that my work can always be described as Christian, but I hope what I write is truthful, whatever it is about, whether that's an adaptation of a biblical book, a piece of social justice, or a show for pure entertainment. I've written plays about child soldiers, knife crime and sex trafficking. Part of that is not just to perform a play about those subjects but to get the audience to engage with an issue and perhaps reflect on their own life.

As part of my work with Roughshod we take shows into prisons. Sometimes we get a bit of heckling, particularly in young offender institutions where there are obviously some people who are quite immature, but often the older inmates will knuckle down on the guys who are trying to upset the show. In high-security prisons we don't have much trouble because generally the prisoners are so grateful that we've come in to see them at all. Often we get an incredible response and I don't just mean in terms of appreciation. We recently toured a show in prisons that had a sketch in it about forgiveness. In the story, a murderer is forgiven by the parents of his victim. At each performance the prisoners listened in complete silence. Afterwards one prisoner told me: 'I've never thought about it like that before. I didn't realise that I could be forgiven.'

In the workshops afterwards I'll often hear the most heart-breaking stories of regret – regret from prisoners about what they've done or what they've realised since they've been put away. It is as though the drama has allowed them to be vulnerable in a way they might not otherwise be, and so be open to change. For others the ideas might sit with them, and who knows, something in them might stir a positive change at another time.

Reward is a regular part of my job, but I try never to take that for granted. A while ago I left my job in theatre to work as a school teacher. Much of my work is with young people, taking a group of four or five actors into schools to encourage learning through interaction and creativity. My degree is in theatre and I have a masters in writing and performance, but I always felt that I wasn't really qualified in educational work. Once I had a family, I thought that perhaps I should get a qualification in education, that teaching might be a more stable occupation for me financially.

I'd always thought that if someone didn't like their job it was because the job was boring or because they weren't very good at it and felt inadequate. Neither was true for me in teaching. It was always great working with young people and there was never a dull day. The standards body, Ofsted, wrote nice things about me and I was offered good jobs by people who wanted to keep me. Parents, young people and staff all said nice things about me and I got great results. Yet in those four years I spent teaching I was immensely unhappy. I learned a lot in that time and realised what I enjoyed about my job in theatre and why I had worked in that area for so long.

Financially it was a big risk to leave teaching, but since I've made the move it's been clear that I made the right decision. In my first year I secured enough freelance work to earn the same amount as I was earning as a teacher. In terms of family life it's much better for us, we're a happier household because I'm happier. I'm using the gifts I've been given and it's exciting. It's taken me a time, but I know now that working in theatre is where I'm meant to be.

3 Living the Gospel

Stuart Petty

Stuart Petty is Lead Anglican Chaplain at York District Hospital.

John Sentamu writes:

Following God is not about doing the right thing; it is about living our lives by gospel values.

It is often said that as Christians we shouldn't just 'talk the talk', but that we should also 'walk the walk'. This doesn't mean that we have to be faultless, it means that we have to be human. Our voice can only be authentic if we judge ourselves by the standards we set others – and vice versa.

To live the Gospel we need to see the humanity in others. We need to recognise the need that exists. It is not always about offering solutions. Sometimes in difficult situations just lending our time, our compassion and a listening ear is what is called for.

In life, we won't always have the answers – but that shouldn't stop us getting alongside people and trying to help when times get tough.

This chapter looks at the story of Stuart, a hospital chaplain, who has learnt that while life is messy and you can never fully control it, your personal experience and simple presence can always help those searching for answers.

✥

A midwife once said about me, 'You'll be all right with him, he's almost human.' I took it as a compliment because I know what she meant, or I think that I do. So many people have a stereotypical view of what a hospital chaplain is going to be like. There can often be a weird perception that I'm going to judge, or that I'm part of a judging church. I think it is important to dispel those myths. If anyone thinks that walking around with a dog collar on is a power trip then they should try it. It means that I'm not anonymous. Everyone knows that I am a chaplain, even if their views of who a chaplain is and what the job involves might not be the reality of who I am or what I do. Saying that, I think it is important for me to wear my dog collar in the hospital so that people see me around. Otherwise, as soon as they see a chaplain, the perception is that something very bad has happened. It also means that people can watch how I work and, hopefully, they might see me and think, he's ok. Perhaps, if they see I'm not so bad, they might even come over and have a word.

Usually I will approach someone and say, 'Hello, I'm Stuart, I'm a chaplain here. May I say hello?' People have every right to say, 'No, not really. I've had a horrible day.' Sometimes, though, people will say to me, 'I don't go to church,' as if that's going to stop me talking to them. I'm not there to proselytise. If someone wants to talk about faith I'll talk about faith, but often the topic of conversation is sparked by something else, like a magazine left on a table or photographs by the bed. Obviously, I'll accept someone saying, 'Go away, I don't want to speak to you,' but I very rarely get people saying, 'What are you doing here?' I think that people almost expect me to be there, in a way. Sometimes they want me to do something, but can't always articulate what. It may be that they want me to say a prayer, or sometimes it's just about sitting with someone in the awfulness.

There's something important about being uncomfortable. I'd be more anxious if someone thought they could start working in a hospital chaplaincy and walk through it. When you get called onto a ward you don't know who you're going to meet. You get ushered behind a curtain and you have no idea of the dynamics, who these people are or what has happened. There are all these questions going on in my head – when do I stay, when do I go, do I say something? I learned fairly early on in the role that my nervousness was leading me to speak when often the most appropriate thing was to sit quietly. I've sat in an intensive care unit with about thirty family members, where actually there's nothing to say, but it's important that I stay there. I had to learn that filling the silence was more my issue. It was about me being uncomfortable. Yet, even in the times when I can't think of anything to say, I'm amazed that God still finds a way to use me. In times when I feel I've had the least to offer, people will still come up to me afterwards and thank me.

There are lots of places where people look for God. Of course you can find him in church or in the Bible, but when we're really open to him we'll see he's everywhere. I am forever finding him in other people. People always amaze me. I love meeting them and listening to their stories. I get to know people at great depth very quickly in a hospital setting because of the nature of what they're going through. I'll get called onto a ward to the bedside of someone who's dying. As I'm sitting there, if it's appropriate, often within a few minutes I'm learning all about this person's life. I'm hearing stories about the family who are gathered round. I might see that person two or three times a day over a period. I feel that I know them and they feel that they know me. OK, we may not understand this encounter, where it's led us or what it means in the great scheme of things, but it's been really precious.

A lot of what happens in a hospital doesn't make sense. The God I try to follow is in that messiness. Of course I wouldn't try to articulate this to a family where something horrible has happened, but I hope that in some small way my presence might enable them to see that God is there in the messiness. That he isn't a God who sends down horrible things. He's a forgiving God, a God who loves us, who doesn't judge, but accepts us.

In an acute healthcare setting things can happen very quickly. Often people I meet are very numb and in complete shock about what's happening. A man recently said to me: 'I believed in God until today. That's it, I'm finished with him.'

When you've got stark things happening you've got every right to be angry and say, 'Where is this God that you purport to follow? Where is he now?' It's for us as Christians to not be afraid to take that risk, to come alongside people and be in those situations where life doesn't make sense. It's about being with people and accompanying them in sometimes horrible areas of their lives and trying to give them another picture of the church, because lots of people have nothing to do with the church.

I haven't got the right answers. I'd never say, I know exactly how you feel, because I can't. Even if I've gone through a similar thing, I can never say that. All I can do is to come alongside. It is about being honest and saying, 'Yes, I doubt too. I get angry with God.' The God I follow doesn't mind you being angry. Sometimes you've every right to be angry. For me, it's about living the Gospel and struggling with it.

Lots of lovely people have horrible things thrown at them and I'm always amazed at how well they hold their life together. Often I am the one who comes away from situations feeling encouraged. I'm encouraged by the way people keep composed after hearing a terrible diagnosis, and by the way they look after each other – the closeness of family and friends. People, often very sacrificially, will come in to visit a relative or friend two or three times a day, sometimes for months. When I see those things, I'm the one left thinking – I don't know how I'd cope in that situation or with that diagnosis. Often they'll say, 'There must be people far worse off than me.' Well, yes, there may well be, but it's what is happening to that person now that is important, yet somehow they can still look to other people, even to me, asking how I am.

People will often say to me, 'How do you do what you do?' It is awful at times, but there are also good times to share and lots of laughter. I'm very happy in a hospital environment. It is a community – I suppose you could think of the hospital as my parish in a way. I worked in a variety of different hospital roles before I became a chaplain. I worked in housekeeping, as a porter and as an auxiliary nurse. I even spent ten months training as a student nurse, but while I loved the ward work I wasn't so good at the theory. It's all been useful though, because it helps me to recognise the validity of all the roles in a hospital. I'm always telling other staff that people won't wait for me to come along in a dog collar before they'll want to discuss something that is worrying them. Patients will see someone working on a ward and get to know them in a way that they'd never think of approaching me. In this sense, I'm just one member of a much bigger team.

It is important to get my role into perspective, because while it is a vocation, I have got a life outside of the hospital and a lot of the time I've got the balance wrong. I'm learning gradually that the hospital runs without me. I'm not indispensable. In fact, the hospital runs really well without me. What I do out-side of work – spending time with my family, going to music gigs, riding my motorbike – it is all part of who I am as a person and I hope adds to what I can offer. If I only spent time in the hospital what experience and stories would I have to share with people? What about the rest of life? I think that God wants us to live our life in fullness as much as we can. I give my best at the hospital but when I'm not in the hospital I try to live that other bit of life that I think God wants me to live as well. It's important to me that I find a balance, although I never get it quite right.

My job does highlight those things in life that are important. Sometimes the trivialities that we worry about, that I worry about, aren't really that important when I see what some people are going through. At the hospital I don't need to be reminded of the importance of the present moment. It's important to make the most of this bit of life that we have here and now, which is really easy to say, but much harder to live. Of course, it is easier to hear myself say those things to others than it is to do them myself. Lots of things I say, about being forgiven, about being loved, about being kind to yourself, if I lived them out, my whole life could be different.

Lots of us have things planned, but life doesn't always happen that way. If anyone thinks they're fully in control of life, I'm not quite sure where they're living. They'd have to be quite unique. Life's not like that – not in my experience, anyway. Life doesn't fit into neat boxes. It's about exploration. It's about the journey.

The other day when I was in the supermarket a man came up to me and asked, 'Are you the vicar from the hospital?' I wasn't dressed as a chaplain, in fact I probably looked like I'd been living rough for about three years, but he still recognised me. 'I just wanted to say, thank you for sticking in with us,' he said. As he walked away I remembered who he was and the upset that his family had gone through. Even in all that pain, he still had a heart to thank those who stood beside him. Those things stay with me. The Emmaus Road is one of my favourite passages. It is a lovely image for me of the risen Lord coming alongside his disciples. He has a word with them and there's a lovely expression – didn't our hearts burn. For me, that is what chaplaincy is all about – coming alongside and feeling our hearts burn.

4   Hope, Life and Transformation

Tim Renshaw

Tim Renshaw manages the Cathedral Archer Project, a day centre that supports the homeless and vulnerable in Sheffield. The majority of the centre's clients are street drinkers, alcoholics and drug users of varying levels. Many are not registered with a local GP and rely on the prescribing nurse at the centre for their medical support.

John Sentamu writes:

It's easy to be judgemental of other people. Do you remember the story in the Bible of the crowd who were going to stone a woman to death because of her adultery? Jesus says: 'Let him who is without sin cast the first stone.'

The reality is we have all done things wrong in our lives, and continue to make mistakes, whoever we are. We are not saved through our own actions and achievements, but rather by God's grace.

If God, the perfect and blameless creator, can find it in his heart to forgive us, then why can't we find it in our hearts to do the same?

So often we make snap judgements about how we think others live their lives based on how something looks, rather than how things are under the surface. Being able to love someone for who they are, without judging them, is so important.

Everyone needs love and understanding and a sense of belonging in their lives. Imagine the feeling we get when we see our extended family at Christmas time, or the sense of pride when we hear our national anthem and see our flag flying at the Olympics. We have an identity that we cherish, it says about where we are from and it informs where we are going.

The same thing is true with God. We all have an identity in him and a sense of belonging in our shared humanity. We are all brothers and sisters in Christ, part of a family at which he is at the head offering us love, support and encouragement.

When we see the lonely, the dispossessed and disenfranchised, we should realise that everyone is loved by God – no one is excluded.

This chapter tells the story of Tim Renshaw, manager of a project caring for the homeless and vulnerable in Sheffield.

❖

When I was thirteen years old, I overheard people telling a story about a mad woman who lived on the street. Then it hit me who they were talking about. She was standing at the gate waving a stick ... yes, that was my grandma.

Since developing dementia, my grandma had started living month on, month off between our house and my uncle's. My mum was very keen to make sure my grandma was comfortable. That meant, someone would have to help her to stand to prevent her getting sores from sitting for too long, and she also needed help feeding. We all had to take our turn in looking after her, and on a Saturday morning, when my parents were at work, it was mine.

When she was eating, my grandma had an uncanny knack of collecting anything pea-sized in the corner of her mouth. After she'd finished her food she'd fish them out again and I'd watch as she balanced them on the end of her tongue and blew them around the room. My dad was incredibly impatient with her. Once her leg wouldn't bend when he was trying to get her into the car. I could sense him getting more and more frustrated. Eventually she bent her leg, but then almost as soon as she did, she straightened it again, right under his chin. I found incidents like this quite funny, but ultimately they were sad, particularly for my dad, because she was still his mum and yet because of her illness it was like she was another person, a stranger living in our house.

I don't know how much these teenage experiences influenced the career path I chose, but I've always found myself working with people on the edge of society in some way. In my twenties I had a job helping adults with learning disabilities achieve greater independence. I'd take people around town, showing them how to do everyday things that most people take for granted, like getting on a bus or buying lunch in a cafe. The idea was, I would be there to support them if they needed me, but at some point they might be able to go out independently and buy lunch for themselves. Invariably someone with Down's syndrome who looked a little bit helpless at a cafe counter would attract someone to carry their tray or whatever. Whenever this happened, I'd butt in straight away. 'No. Clear off,' I'd tell them. 'Go away. This person needs to do it themselves.'

My intention was good. I wanted to see people's lives change for the better, but perhaps I was a little over-zealous about how I went about it. Looking back, if I was doing that same job now, I hope I'd be a lot more accepting. Somebody reaching out to help might not always be the best thing for the person who is learning to be independent, but if that help is well intended then that's not a bad thing for society and I'd hate to lose that charitable spirit.

It's taken a long time, but I think I've become more patient about allowing people to be people. To enjoy what they are offering where they are. I'm fascinated by the ideas of judgement and non-judgement, and what we mean by being non-judgemental, because however we live we are making judgements of some sort every moment of the day. I suppose, what we often mean by non-judgemental is being able to take somebody with all their faults and embracing who they are and what they bring. In a sense, that is how I try to think about the work that I do now at the Cathedral Archer Project.

The project started in 1990 as a breakfast club and has since grown to encompass all types of support to help people find pathways away from homelessness and exclusion. Initially it was a faith-based project and, although it is now independent of the cathedral, it still has the ethos of the people who founded it. There are still people working within it who are practising Christians, but most of the staff aren't and the clientele could be anyone. There is nothing within the centre itself that marks it as a faith-based project, but there is something special, I think, about being based at the cathedral.

When I go to work, I enjoy the contrast of the cathedral and the centre. The cathedral is quiet and meditative. There is order, sung evening prayer, polished furniture and people speaking in hushed tones. Then I walk through the doors to the centre and people might be grumpy, loud and annoyed. They could be showering or having their teeth drilled, or doing art, or playing the guitar. It is so different, yet somehow it feels right that it should be contained within this church establishment. There's something very real about a place of worship and prayer offering concern and support – a church that has people at its doorstep, looking in, wondering how life might be different and at the same time welcoming them within it in a very practical way.

It's very easy to look at something like homelessness and make the point that if these people had made different decisions along the way, or had the strength to say no at certain times, then their lives would be very different. I've made so many mistakes in my life and they haven't taken me to homelessness. Why shouldn't I be patient with other people who are making mistakes, as I sometimes have, and still am? It is difficult to be in a position where you are making mistakes yourself and still condemn someone for making any number of mistakes, especially when you look at the demographics of a problem like homelessness. Most people who find themselves in this situation come from poorer backgrounds where there wasn't a value placed on education, or because of family circumstances they fell out of school and possibly got involved in crime early as well. They often have a lot of barriers to get over in life and feel that they don't have the resources or support that they can trust at the time to help overcome them. Yes, there is a lot of help and support out there, but whether people can feel they can invest or hope in it is an entirely different matter.

It can be very easy to distance ourselves from people who are outside many of the normal things we take for granted, like banking, housing and health. To try to give people a tiny glimpse of what life might be like on the streets we sometimes organise sleepouts at the cathedral. Of course, compared to sleeping rough it is a very domesticated experience. The toilets are open and coffee is available all night long. However, the experience of not being able to sleep for most of the night is not one that most people would like to repeat. In the morning we ask them, how do you get on the phone to deal with benefits or housing? Are you in the best place to deal with that? Once we start asking questions people soon realise that being homeless isn't an easy place to be, and if that is where you are, it isn't an easy place to get out of either.

There are many things about homelessness that people never think about, like boredom for instance. There is no sense of routine, of doing regular activities like showering, eating, washing-up, watching TV and going to bed at particular times.

Being on the streets with nothing to do and nowhere to go is boring, so what do people do in that situation? They probably drink. If you sleep rough as a one-off there is a sense of people watching you all the time because you look rough, and it is disconcerting. The people we work with at the centre have got used to that, and that is part of the problem. They have started to live like outsiders. Living on the streets is not a matter of survival for them any more; it's a habit of life.

For most people living on the streets rejection is a regular part of life. When they come to a centre like ours being cared for and supported creates such a powerful memory that they often refer to it as the first time that anyone has ever treated them with any decency. To overcome that deep sense of rejection and begin to change their self-image takes a long time. There are many centres like ours up and down the country. Some people who turn their lives around have travelled, using several centres for support. Eventually they start to think differently because, actually that place treated me ok, and that other place treated me ok too. One man told me how his motivation to stop taking drugs was probably down to the cumulative effect of going to different centres and meeting different people who were affirming. In this way I'm just joining in a line of people who are being encouraging in that sort of way.

As an organisation like ours grows, I am also aware that it can be easy for me to become removed from the daily work of the project. For this reason I spend an hour-and-a-half manning the centre's reception desk every Monday morning. I know that I'm the worst person at that job and I make a lot of mistakes, but I like doing it because it means that I get to know people, I recognise their faces, I can ask their names and hear their stories. It helps me to understand the project better, but it is also part of the delight of the job.

Homelessness can seem incredibly negative, but sometimes sitting in the centre with people who are in that community can be a laugh. It's not a wonderfully healthy way of living, but it's not without its good points. The people there might not want to be in that place, but they've got friends and people they can share things with. Even though I know that I'm going to go home and they might be just wasting time until they can get into some accommodation, if they can find any place to stay at all, the time we spend chatting is still a joyful and enjoyable encounter.

I have seen changes in my own life, so hopefully I treat people with the same understanding that change is possible and where they are at the moment, well, that's not too bad either. If you are on the streets at this particular moment in time and doing some of the things that will help you get accommodation, then there are worse places to be. If you've got accommodation and are looking to get more permanent accommodation, then look at what you've done to be able to get to that place.

Of course, I know that life on the streets is not the best life in the world, it's not best for the people who are homeless or for the local communities in which they live, so at the centre we want to provide opportunities to change that. But unless we accept where people are in the first place, there can be no communication; there is no platform from which to move forward. It's about knowing what you can and can't change, particularly when you're dealing with people.

Some of the people who volunteer in the centre have come from homeless backgrounds, so we work with a lot of people who have made the change and are making it. As I get older, I still want the world to change and I still like to see positive changes in people's lives, but it's not the main motivator for what I do. If it was, then I'd probably think less of those people who are not making any progress, and I don't. There will always be people on the outside in some sort of way, it's part of life. To me, the most important thing now is to be there for them.

5 Hearing God's Call

Lyn Edwards

Lyn Edwards is founder of Shackles Off youth project, a registered charity in Seascale, Cumbria, which provides support to empower young people to make a positive and fuller contribution to the local community and to society.

John Sentamu writes:

Can you remember what you dreamt about last night? Some people have very vivid dreams that stay with them for a long time; others couldn't tell you a single thing that happened.

Whilst most dreams are probably our brains trying to process information and thoughts from what has gone before, there is little doubt that God sometimes uses dreams to get messages across.

In the book of Joel, God says that he will pour his Spirit out onto his servants, both men and women. Old men will dream dreams, and young men will see visions.

God knows us better than we know ourselves and is constantly reaching out to us, sometimes in ways which we don't readily understand. What we have to do is listen, discern what is being said, and then embrace the vision wholeheartedly.

There is a well-known story called 'Footprints'. It is a parable about how a man looks at his life's walk along a very long beach – and God walks alongside him. For most parts of the journey there are two sets of footprints, but in sections where times were tough there is only one set of footprints.

Troubled by this, the man says to God: 'You said that if I followed you, then you would always walk with me through thick and thin. In looking back, I see that during the most painful times there is only one set of footprints. Why did you leave me when I needed you the most?'

God replies: 'I love you and would never leave you. It was during those times in your journey, when you suffered the most, that I carried you.'

This chapter looks at the story of Lyn, a woman who embraced God's vision by moving to a new town with her husband and setting up a youth project, getting alongside people going through tough times, following God's call to show love in action.

I don't say that I hear God's voice easily. I don't think any of us do. So, when I tell you that I sold my house and moved more than three hundred miles north to set up a project for young people, because God called me to do it, it is because I have no doubt in my mind that he did.

It all started in September 2005. I had just retired from teaching. My husband had been very ill and then I had gotten ill with what the doctors thought at the time was lupus, but now the diagnosis shifts between that and rheumatoid arthritis. It had been a long time since we'd had a holiday together, so we were delighted when a friend gave us a gift of money to go off somewhere. We decided to put the money in the car and headed up to Cumbria to visit friends.

It was lovely to get away, catch up with old friends, walk along the beach and plan how we were going to enjoy our retirement. Then over two nights I had the most vivid dreams. My husband would often wake and tell me about dreams that he'd had, but it was something I never did. Obviously I must have dreamed, but I'd never been able to recall one until that night. I can still picture it now. There was a young man playing a guitar and singing the song 'Shackles' – 'take the shackles off my feet, I just want to praise you'. Then I was walking down a road I didn't recognise and there were all these young people, with heads bowed, dragging chains behind them. I heard a voice say, 'Who will tell them of a God that loves them and a saviour who cares?' It was the voice I knew. The voice that had been with me all my life, but something inside told me that this time it was God speaking. The following night I had another dream. This time I was in my car driving into a village. I parked up and could smell the sea and hear the waves crashing on the shore. I looked across to a row of shops and houses, on the corner was a cafe with a sign above the door with the writing 'Shackles Off' next to an image of broken chains. It was the only building with a light on, so I went in and there was my friend, the one I had gone to Cumbria to visit, serving behind a counter, while young people sat around chatting. On the counter was a prayer box. I picked it up and took it to some elderly people, asking them to pray about the prayers that were in it. I had no idea what these dreams meant, but they were so out of the ordinary for me that initially I didn't share them with anyone.

The following Sunday my friend suggested that we go to a church in the next village. It was a couple of miles away, but, because she knows that I'm not exactly traditional when it comes to worship, she thought that the service there might suit me better. As we drove I recognised the road as being the place I'd driven down in my dream. We parked up and there on the corner was the shop, except it was old and tatty, and looked like it had been closed and uncared for, for a long time. I couldn't believe it. I'd never been to this place in my life, so how could I have seen these things? I told my friend about the dreams. 'Wow,' she said excitedly, 'I've often walked past that very corner shop and thought, God, wouldn't it be lovely if you did something there.' To me her words felt like God was confirming through other people that my thoughts were of him.

The next day, I went for a walk on the beach with my husband and told him. I knew that it would sound mad because I'd just retired and we were going to be doing things differently, taking life a little easier. Yet, here I was talking about moving half way across the country to set up a project for young people. I didn't quite know what that would involve, apart from it being something that would remove the chains of worry and stress that can stop young people from being the whole person God wants them to be – giving them the freedom to find purpose, fulfilment, security and success.

'Are you sure it's from God?' my husband asked.

'I think it is.'

'OK,' he said. 'We'll do it.'

We put our house up for sale as soon as we got home to Pembroke, and within five months we'd moved and set up home in Seascale, the village I'd seen in my dream.

In my work as a teacher I headed up a behavioural unit, specialising in those on the edge, who misbehaved. My husband always had a heart for those on the outside too. As a young man in his teens and early twenties he had been homeless, living on the streets. He was living on the margins of society, he was involved in the drug culture and even had a prison record. Then at his brother's wedding God touched his heart and he turned his life around. Although not as extreme, I'd had my own struggles too. I grew up at the wrong end of town. My father was Greek and because he spoke broken English most people assumed he was ignorant, even though he was a professor. No one at school expected much of me educationally. I had to fight to be a teacher, but I refused to believe that God would put something on my heart if I couldn't do it.

In many ways my husband and I had both seen God do the impossible. Throughout our lives, most of the situations we'd found ourselves involved in didn't have easy answers. Unless God moved, there was nothing we could do, but we believed that if God had said it was possible then it was. We knew first hand that God goes places that people would shy away from, that he loves people whom others might not want in their homes, and he can make changes in situations that many people would think impossible.

When we first moved to Seascale, apart from my friend, we knew nobody. I knew what, ideally, I'd like to do, but where to start? I went along to the church in the village, the one my friend had taken me to those months before we moved. I don't remember much about the service, other than there were no young people – where were they? Just as I felt like giving up, the organist started to play the hymn 'One More Step Along the World I Go'. I don't cry easily, but I started to sob, so much that an elderly woman approached me afterwards and invited me downstairs for a coffee. I recognised the place she took me to from my dream. It was where I had taken the prayer box at the end. Here we go again, I thought, even the church is here, I guess I'll have to carry on.

I knew where I wanted to be, but I didn't know where to start to get there. So, I started by praying. I'd see young people getting off school buses as I was driving along, they'd pass me on the street or walk by my window. I didn't know any of them, but I prayed for them all the same. I prayed for them because I didn't know what else to do. Then, I started to get involved in the church, running prayer groups and organising events. Hope 2008 came along, which was a nationwide project to encourage local churches to put their faith into action in the communities in which they lived. I volunteered to be the Hope champion for Seascale. I thought, if the Pope can have a Popemobile then we can have a Hopemobile, and that's what we did. We got a car, and drove round to where the young people were, offering drinks and crisps, chatting and building relationships. At first they were a bit suspicious, but once they got to know us a trust started to build. By the end of the month everyone in the village knew who I was and would say hello. From there it snowballed. Suddenly these young people were my young people. I knew them by name, I knew where they lived, I knew what they got up to. They'd even shown me their hideaways where all sorts of things happened. If any of the young people needed someone to go to court with them, or meet their family if there had been a problem, I went with them. I couldn't give up on them because I had a relationship, and when you have a relationship you can't let people go.

It was more than two years since we'd moved from Pembroke. Most days I walked past the old, tattered shop, and it felt like madness. I was no closer to doing anything with that shop or figuring out how I could. Then one Saturday morning a friend called me: 'Lyn, there's something happening at the shop, you ought to go down there.'

After years of neglect the premises was getting a makeover, fresh paintwork inside and out, central heating, a new kitchen. My heart sank. An old friend from Pembroke told me not to worry, that the shop was being done up for me, but I wasn't so sure. 'You ought to go and speak to the man, see what he's doing,' she said.

I knocked on the door, 'Can I have five minutes?' I asked.

The man invited me in and I told him my story, about why I'd moved to Seascale.

'Well, I don't even believe in God,' he smiled. 'But if you've sold up your property and moved here because of my property I'll let you rent it. I was going to put it on the market this afternoon, but if you can find the money to rent it, it's yours.'

I didn't know how I would pay for it, but told myself if I found one hundred people to give me a pound a week for a year, then we'd have enough.

Now there is a sign above the door which reads 'Shackles Off', above an image of broken chains. When we first started I could never have envisaged it growing in the way it has. I thought that we were just going to be a drop-in centre, with coffee tables and chairs, where young people could stop off for a chat. As soon as we opened our doors I realised that we needed to be much more than that. Some young people had huge problems – they didn't have jobs, they didn't have qualifications, they were in trouble with the law, they had health problems. Even the bright ones were worried about UCAS. Where did all this come from? I couldn't just serve a cup of coffee and send them on their way.

Through the centre we have helped homeless young people find shelter, we've worked alongside those with drug and alcohol addictions, and encouraged those with mental health problems, including self-harm, to seek the help they need. We have a fantastic team of volunteers and a full-time youth worker and project development officer. Together we do a phenomenal amount that I could never achieve alone. My heart is still on the streets, and for those who don't come into our premises, I'll go out to them.

My husband recently passed away. He was fifty-eight. What will I do without him? Where will I go? I have no idea, but the God who has remained faithful throughout my life will always be with me. I trust in him completely and know that he doesn't finish with us until we breathe our last breath. There is so much more work for God's church to do here on earth. He wants the best for us and it doesn't matter what appears to be standing in the way, he will help us to get through it, one way or another. The Gospel is real, and sometimes that means having the confidence in God to stand up when everything looks a mess and say, 'But God has said so, I'm telling you that we are going to do this, we will not be defeated.'

6 Challenging Stereotypes

Ben Norton

Ben Norton is a pioneer minister based at St Cuthbert's church in Marton, Teesside. A trained hairdresser, Ben volunteers his skills one day a week in a local salon, in an effort to meet more people and become a more approachable face of the church.

John Sentamu writes:

Let's get one thing straight, you don't need to wear a clerical collar to serve God.

It doesn't matter what job God is asking you to do, the key thing is to remember that he is in charge and that the rest of us are just in service.

For example, it makes no difference if I am Sentamu – father, or Sentamu – lawyer, or Sentamu – parish priest, or Sentamu – archbishop; my call is to follow Jesus wherever he may lead. I hope you feel the same way about your own life.

Too often we put our own personal ambitions, desires and expectations above what God wants for us. Part of our role is to listen to God's call and serve wherever we are needed. Make space for others to travel with you on the journey. Remember you can't always see faith growing until you take a step back.

We don't have to be in church to have conversations about faith; that can happen anywhere.

This chapter looks at the story of Ben, a pioneer minister who volunteers one day a week in his local hairdressers so that he can be at the heart of his local community. Listening to people, where they are, is at the heart of his work.

❖

Some people think that when I grow up I'll be a proper vicar. I'm not sure I know what that means for me. Whether I wear my dog collar or not, I'm just Ben. My heart and my passion is about allowing people to see who Jesus is. My faith is who I am. If someone I know is ill and I pop round with a card, would I do that as a priest, yes. Would I do that as a friend, I probably would too. Forget being a priest, just as a Christian I would care for people, journey with them and pray for them. The boundaries are grey, but I find that exciting.

My faith really came alive when I was in my late teens. I remember very clearly praying, 'I trust you with everything I've got. Whatever you ask of me, God, I'll do.' That's been my promise all the way through. At the time I was training to be a hairdresser. I remember going into the shop one day with a huge cross around my neck – I was full of it. I could die with embarrassment thinking back to how I must have come across at that time. Yet, saying that, my behaviour created an interesting dynamic. It wasn't that I was always preaching, but I didn't hide my faith, and it was interesting how people reacted to that. I started getting a lot of questions about what I believed and other people started telling me where they were at with their faith.

I find people's questions helpful, because they make me think more deeply about what I believe and why I believe it. It also helps me to get rid of all the other rubbish that can cloud my thinking and helps me to really clarify my views. Wearing a dog collar magnifies that experience, so those types of conversations are more frequent for me these days. Now it is all part of the job, but I would do it anyway. It is who I am. The fact that the church is allowing me to do it without having to do a different job is fantastic. Of course, at times it is difficult and I don't always get it right, but I'm privileged to be able to do what I do.

Initially, I put off ordination because, at twenty-six years old, I thought that I needed to be a lot older, wiser and have more life experience behind me. At this time I'd left hairdressing, had studied at theological college and was working in youth ministry. I spent a fantastic five years working in youth ministry, but as my contract was coming to an end I wasn't sure what was next for me. In my mind being a vicar was very different to being a youth minister. I was talking about this to my vicar, about how I might be interested in offering for ordination one day, a day when I would be old and grey, and know a lot more than I did then.

'Maybe you can push that door now,' he said.

'But I don't want to be a vicar and I don't want to run a church,' I insisted.

Then he told me about how the Church of England was exploring Fresh Expressions of church and it sounded interesting. It was about the time when the new ministry guidelines were going through the House of Bishops to encourage vocations to pioneer ministry as a recognised focus of ordained ministry. I went to see the bishop and explained how I was feeling and it went from there.

Now I am ordained, so I am a vicar, but while I'm connected to a church, I'm not in charge of it. My role is a pioneer minister, someone who works for the Church of England, usually in a parish setting, working alongside the inherited church, but who is given the brief and the scope to pioneer fresh expressions of church with people who aren't in church and begin to explore their faith journey with them.

I work with the vicar of St Cuthbert's, so there are things to help out with, like communion services and planning for Sundays, but I don't have the restriction of being responsible for running the church. Part of my role is to work with people who maybe don't go to church or maybe haven't thought through their faith. That means going out into the community and meeting people where they are. It means being creative with my own view of church and maybe doing things a little bit differently, like renting a beach hut on the run up to Christmas to create a live advent calendar on the sea front, or holding a religious discussion group in a pub.

A lot of the time, I think it is about culturally reconnecting people to faith and then discovering what the church means in that cultural context. I've got a young family and my wife works, so if I didn't do the job that I do, I'm not sure that I would go to church on a Sunday. That's not because I wouldn't want to, but just because of the way that lifestyles are these days.

My job gives me the opportunity to help build community, and preach the Gospel in a way that is culturally relevant and is heard. It's incredible. The responsibility is absolutely beyond me. Sometimes I think, 'If you knew who I am!', but that's the core of preaching, we have to keep our feet on the ground and keep balanced because it is beyond us, and we need every ounce of God's strength to be able to do it. What excites me so much about doing this work within the Church of England, is that I am privileged to have all of this heritage behind me that allows me to do my job in a way that's not just wacky and out there, and has no ties to anything else. Without having the stability of the parish and everything that goes with traditional church, it could be quite easy for me to lose my focus.

I've recently moved to the parish I'm in now. I'm new to the area, so to try to get to know some people I decided to use my old skills and volunteer one day a week at a hairdressers. At first having a vicar cut hair was a bit of a novelty. I attracted a bit of attention in the local press and the shop cut out a newspaper article about me and stuck it on the front desk, so everyone coming in knew my other job. The staff all took it in good spirits and have been great. When I'm there, I'm just a hairdresser the same as anyone else. That's the job I'm doing. I don't wear my dog collar, in fact, I don't bring up being a vicar at all unless someone asks. That's not to say that I won't talk about it. I will and I do. The topic usually comes up naturally because of the newspaper article on the front desk, or else my boss, who works cutting hair next to me, will tell people, 'He's a vicar', and the conversation goes from there.

It's great to be in a place that's not church to begin to have those conversations. Although generally people don't ask me much about being a vicar while I'm cutting their hair. People don't always know what to make of it, many probably think that we're having them on. Longevity will be the key because it takes a while to develop any kind of relationship.

It's the same in any new setting, I tend to find that people want me to know where they are at with their faith. The conversation usually starts with them telling me what they believe and then asking me what I think about different issues. People ask me questions all the time that I don't have the answers to, but I think that's the joy of faith. It's not all black and white. For me it's about the journey.

Listening is the key. Not everyone wants answers, but everyone wants to be heard and everyone wants their values to be recognised. A lot of the time people think that their world view will clash with the church, or that their lifestyle will clash with the church, or any number of things they think will clash with the church. For this reason they often push church and faith aside. Life isn't as black and white as that and that's where stuff begins to happen. My role is about listening to where people are at and accepting whatever views or beliefs they do have. When people find that whatever world view they have is accepted, that allows them to begin to journey in their faith.

Through being more open I've seen all sorts of different people awaken their spiritual journey. I used to run a lads' church that sometimes looked like what we might recognise as church and other times was nothing like it. One chap came along and for a month he just told us his life story. As we all listened something amazing began to happen. No one had ever listened to him before, but as he realised he was being listened to, really listened to, he started to open up more, he started to trust, and friendships were built. I don't know where that chap is now with his faith, but I'd certainly say that he is more open now and that he's on the journey.

While I was involved in the lad's club another chap asked if he could come and spend some time with the group. He was doing a PhD on Fresh Expressions of church. He didn't take part, but he sat in on the meetings that we had and chatted to some of the other lads involved. At the end of it all he collated all his information, and told us what he'd observed. He said that during the time he spent with us, everyone he interviewed had moved one step along in their faith. So, if they described themselves as atheist they would now identify as agnostic, if they were agnostic, they would now call themselves theists, or if they were theists to start with they would now say they were Christian.

The research picked up changes that I hadn't always noticed were happening. When you are doing any kind of work with people you don't always notice changes that happen over a period of time. I suppose in one way, it's like watching kids grow up. Aunts and uncles who haven't seen them for a while will comment on how they've grown, but the parents who look at them every day don't see a huge change. It's the same with faith. You can't always see faith grow until you take a step back. Suddenly you realise that someone's world view has changed, the way in which they conduct themselves has changed, or the way they relate to others has changed. When that happens, you know that faith is growing and you can see it.

7   *Trusting God*

Matt Woodcock

The Revd Matt Woodcock is a pioneer minister at Holy Trinity Church in Hull, where he lives with his wife and two young daughters.

John Sentamu writes:

Cynicism is the disease of our modern society. Sadly it has become fashionable not only to criticise the contributions of others, but also question the motivation that moves them to take action, whilst others stand idly by.

If we want to see real change in our communities we have to get out there and take action. We have to put our money where our mouth is and get stuck in.

I never understand people who say they won't speak out on issues that are political. My reasoning for this is threefold: First, everything is political, at least in part – from the state of the streets to the state of the local hospital – nothing exists in isolation.

Secondly, there are no areas in which God's voice should not be heard and into which he cannot reach. Thirdly, if we do not speak out about what we do think, someone will simply speak for us.

But more than this, I think of the words of St Francis of Assisi: 'Preach the Gospel. If necessary, use words.'

If we want to see real transformation we need to stop moaning and start doing. Let us live out the Gospel in our actions and deeds, not just in our words.

Maybe there are things we see around us that could be done better. Could they be done by us? If so, get on and do it. Could things be improved by us offering our help and support? If so, let's get on and do this.

One thing is for sure, very little gets improved by us criticising others without offering practical solutions.

This chapter looks at the story of Matt, a man who was challenged to get off the sidelines and start making a difference.

❖

I'll never forget telling my editor that I was leaving to work for the church. He laughed so hard that tears streaked his cheeks. I know how strange it must have sounded to him at the time. When I first walked in the room he'd assumed I'd been poached by another newspaper, because, without meaning to sound arrogant, I was going places in my career. I loved the job. I loved the adrenaline of the newsroom and the daily battles to come back with the best story. Journalism was all I'd ever wanted to do, yet as I handed over my resignation letter I'd never felt more sure of any decision in my life.

Rewind a couple of years and you might be laughing along with my editor too. On a Sunday you'd always find me sat at the back of church, complaining about how rubbish the service was and bringing the vibe down. I was a journalist. My life was exciting, dynamic and fun. In comparison church was boring. Everyone there was nice, but I wanted to feel something a bit more real. Instead, I just found the whole experience very, very

dull. Then one day a youth worker said to me: 'To be honest,
I'm sick of you moaning. Either leave or do something about it.'
She challenged me to start my own service, using my skills as a
journalist to interview members of the congregation, finding
out about their stories and what made them tick. I liked the idea
– it was kind of Michael Parkinson/Jonathan Ross meets *Songs
of Praise*. So, I took her up on it, we got an old battered sofa,
invited some people to be interviewed and The Lounge was
started. At first we attracted about fifteen people, then the
numbers grew very quickly – all people like me who found
church boring. I couldn't believe it, I was in church and people
were laughing, having a good time and getting involved. It was
amazing. I really began to care about what it meant to be part
of a church community, and as I put more energy into it, slowly
but surely, my church life became as enjoyable as my journalis-
tic life. So, when my vicar asked if I'd ever thought about
working for the church I didn't hesitate. It was a eureka
moment. As soon as I heard his words I absolutely knew it was
what I was going to do and that it was what God wanted for
me.

Of course, the vicar's suggestion wasn't that straightforward. He said that he'd give me a little bit of money, but I'd have
to raise the rest myself. My wife and I had just taken on a
mortgage based on my salary as a journalist. I had a glazed look
in my eyes when I got home. My wife had seen it before so she
knew I was serious when I said: 'I think I've got to leave
journalism and work for the church.' The colour drained from
her face, but, bless her, she didn't try to talk me out of it, 'Well,
if you think that it's from God,' she said, 'then there's nothing
we can do.' I wrote to ten different people whom I hoped might
support me, and all of them wrote back and agreed. Within a
month, I had raised the money I needed to make it work, the
parochial church council agreed and I became their evangelist.
On my first day I looked out at the empty pews. What did
evangelists do? I had no idea.

There is a scene in one of the Indiana Jones movies where
the hero steps out onto an invisible bridge. He believes it is

there but he knows that he is going to have to walk on it to test that out. Everything in his soul says to make the step, even though it looks like he could fall to his death. To me, that's what it's like to trust God. We can't always see where the next step will take us, or even if there will be anything to walk on if we take it. It's hard and he'll push us to our limits, but God meets us in our weakness all the time, and he won't push us beyond what we can do. Saying that, it hasn't become any easier just because I'm an ordained vicar. Taking that risk and learning to trust God is still a daily struggle for me. I don't claim to have the answers. All I can say is, this is what Jesus has done in my life and I believe that he can do the same for you, but you've got to find that out for yourself.

I see too many battered old noticeboards outside churches with nothing on them. Is this a community taking pride in who it is and what it believes? Surely Christians should be communicating the good news, but so often it's as though we are treating the Gospel like bad news because we don't want to tell anyone about it. Of course, it's easier for me to talk about God, because I'm the one in the dog collar, I'm the God man. It would be stranger if I didn't ask, 'Where are you with God?' If someone answers, 'I don't believe a word of it,' then I won't push it, but interestingly I don't get many people saying that. Often the question will spark a conversation. Increasingly I've come to realise that the majority of the population never go near a church unless it is for a christening, wedding or funeral. I've got a heart for those people. God wants to be a part of their lives too, but sometimes people have to feel like they belong before they can believe.

Our church is a beautiful big old building, but that alone won't bring people in. We can't sit there thinking that people will come to us because they won't and they aren't. As a pioneer minister my job is to reach out into the community, to try to break down these barriers that have built up between people and church, and hopefully in so doing also remove any barriers that people perceive between themselves and God.

Sometimes that means doing things differently, but I don't always get it right. For my first sermon at Holy Trinity I took a big risk. It was Harvest Festival, one of the biggest services of the year and there must have been about a thousand people in the congregation, including the Lord Mayor, dignitaries and the leader of the council.

'Are you sure you want me to do it?' I asked my boss.

'Yeah,' he said coolly. 'We've got all these kids in and we need to do something different.'

'How different?'

'Really different.'

So, I started thinking – for many of the people at the service this would be the only time they stepped foot in a church all year. What could I do to make it memorable? How could I ensure this was one church service they wouldn't forget in a hurry?

At Holy Trinity we have the highest pulpit I've ever seen in my entire life, with a huge wide staircase leading up to it. I was preaching on Zacchaeus. My idea was to get the vicar to come out and say, 'Zacchaeus come down for tea,' at which point the organist would play the theme from *Mission Impossible* and I'd climb out of the pulpit and down a ladder onto a box in the middle of the congregation. I'd finish the sermon from there, to emphasise how Jesus doesn't stay distant but comes right into our lives. It all sounded great in theory, but when it came to it I climbed out of the pulpit and the ladder didn't quite reach the top. So, there I was, my arms dangling from the pulpit while my feet were trying to find the ladder. There was an audible gasp as the congregation wondered if I was going to fall. I realise now what I did was stupid and it could have killed me, but I don't regret it. How much good it did I don't know, but I felt that I needed to take a risk because I didn't want the congregation feeling they knew what to expect, I didn't want them to be bored. Of course, some people weren't happy with what I did. They thought that it was disrespectful. Sometimes you've just got to do stuff that ruffles a few feathers, and I'm lucky that I've got a brilliant boss who gives me licence to go for it.

People are always looking for a secret formula for how to get more people involved in the church, but there is no one answer, God does different things in different places. I prayed hard about what I could do. If people weren't going to come to us, then I'd go to them. Opposite the church is a pub called, 'The Mission'. I didn't think a service in a pub would be the answer, but it might be one answer.

I told the landlord and landlady about my idea and they agreed to let me do whatever I wanted on a Sunday. So, I used my journalist contacts to get a bit of publicity and decided to start a service once a month at four o'clock on a Sunday afternoon, which I called 'Full', based on John's gospel where Jesus says, 'I have come in order that you might have life – life in all its fullness.'

Obviously, 'Full' wasn't going to be your traditional church service, but it still needed to be faithful in prayer and faithful to the teachings of Jesus. I wanted to do this in a way that anyone could understand, in a way that rooted scripture firmly in people's everyday lives, without all the churchy language that some people find alienating.

It was easy to get enthused at the organisational stage. There was so much room to be creative. I decided that we'd do notices in the style of a news bulletin, there would be music, videos, interviews, even a popular culture quiz called. Beat the Vicar, where the winner would get a t-shirt with big writing across the front, 'I beat the vicar at Full'.

The day of the first service arrived. Five minutes before we were due to start I was sitting in the pub with my team from the church and no one else. Why did I think this was going to work? What was I doing? I didn't want to be there. I wanted to be in a mega-church with hundreds of other people like me. I didn't need this, whatever this was. I found myself, like I so often do in times of vulnerability, clinging to God, praying, Lord help me, because I can't do this on my own.

I was about to give up for the day when a guy walked in. Years ago he thought he might believe in something so he had gone along to a church service, but when he opened the hymn book he didn't have a clue what the words meant. The vicar started talking but he might as well have been talking a foreign language for all this man understood. To him, church felt like a club that he wasn't invited to. He walked out angry and never went back. Fast-forward a few years and this same man is at the hospital waiting for the birth of his child. Suddenly there are complications. He sees the faces of the doctors – they are worried. They whisk his little son off to an incubator. It doesn't look good. He prays to God, like so many do in desperate circumstances, and makes a deal: 'Right, God, if my son gets better I promise I will go to church. Amen.' His son gets better, and he's so thrilled that tears of joy fill his eyes. Later, as the baby is falling asleep he notices a copy of the *Hull Daily Mail* on the table. He opens it and looking out from the page is my smiling face with a quote underneath, 'Matt Woodcock has just set up a church for people who don't do church.' The man smiles to himself, 'Ok God, I can see you've got a sense of humour. I'll give it a go.'

Sometimes I'll wonder if I'm doing the right thing and then I'll see a life change. Now we get about sixty people coming along to each one of our pub services. I'm also finding that some people who come along want to know more, and in that way our pub service has become a bridge into traditional church.

I write these good things down in a diary because when I'm having a rubbish day it can be so easy to forget why I do what I do. I could talk for hours telling stories about people I've encountered who have promised to come to things and then haven't or have said they'll do something and they haven't. Often life can feel uncomfortable, but I'm learning to trust God to take control of my journey, and every time I do he sets me off on the most remarkable adventure. I let God in and he transformed me from the inside out. He never fails to stir me, to change me, and to help me to be a better person. I'm just blown away by Christ and I can't stop telling people about it – there's no life like it.

8   *Making a Difference through Love*

Richard Nihill

Richard Nihill is an RE teacher and lay chaplain at
Archbishop Holgate School in York. Every two years
he takes a group of schoolchildren to Cape Town in
South Africa, as part of an educational visit which
includes community work and building lasting
relationships between young people in the two
countries.

John Sentamu writes:

*Sometimes in life we need to be challenged about the things that
we value and the direction we are heading. There is no point in
travelling at top speed if you've got the wrong destination in your
sat nav!*

Too often in our lives we focus on the things that are close to us, rather than getting the bigger picture in perspective. We should remember that God's love stretches across international boundaries.

In today's world, we need to ask 'Who is my neighbour?' Is it the person living on our street; someone in the next town; or a person suffering on the other side of the globe?

It is wonderful that modern communications make it easier to follow what is happening in difficult situations around the world, but we still need to have the willingness and the passion to speak out against unfairness and to work together to tackle injustice.

Although small actions make a big difference, when we are united in our goal we can often see change happen more rapidly.

This chapter looks at the story of Richard, an RE teacher who as part of his work-experience regularly takes parties of young people from his school to South Africa to see how others live. Meeting those with different needs to their own, and being able to volunteer practical assistance, has left a lasting legacy for young people on both sides of the world.

When I'm teaching RE, I always tell young people that a big part of faith is rolling your sleeves up and getting stuck in. Like the parable of the sheep and the goats, living out your faith is asking, what can I do to make someone's life better? It's a belief I've always held, but I travelled half-way across the world before I really understood what it meant.

I could live my whole life in the UK and not really notice need. Of course there is need here, but for many years it had been easy to turn my eyes from it. Then I visited South Africa, where poverty stared me full in the face. I couldn't avoid the need right there in front of me, and once I'd seen it, as a Christian, I wanted to respond. At the same time, I knew that if the need was there, the need was here too, albeit in a different way. The question for me then became, in a very real sense, what am I doing about it?

In many ways, from a young age, God had placed South Africa on my heart. When I was at school I watched the film, *Cry Freedom*, about the founder of the black consciousness movement, Steve Biko, and his relationship with a white journalist, Donald Woods. I'd been aware of the struggles to end the apartheid regime, but the film opened my eyes to what was happening in a way that made it more real to me. Suddenly I was politically conscious of the situation in a way that I hadn't been before.

I was at university when South Africa got its first democratic elections in 1994. As its people were going to the polls, I organised a prayer evening through the Christian Union, and in the foolish, rash way students often do, I sent off a fax to the then Archbishop of Cape Town, Desmond Tutu, telling him that he was in our prayers and we hoped everything went well. A couple of days later I received a return fax from the Archbishop. In it he said that it was great we were an ecumenical group praying for the elections and that those prayers were really valued. I was bowled over at the response.

Later my aunt bought me Desmond Tutu's book, *The Rainbow People of God*, about the church's part in the struggle against apartheid. I suppose in some way his life became a symbol of hope for mine, of how we can reach out to help each other, and how great change can occur.

It was a decade later when the opportunity came for me to visit South Africa. It was part of an educational project to build better links between the twinned dioceses of York and Cape Town. I travelled with a couple of colleagues and we visited schools, collecting teaching resources. It was only supposed to be a one-off visit, but when we got there the faith of the people, the welcome we received and the beauty of the place just blew us away.

Our first thoughts were that it was all very well us talking about our visit, but we needed to get some young people out there to experience South Africa for themselves. From there, the idea just took off. Why don't we take a group out in work-experience fortnight? Why don't we go out and do some community work? The more we thought about it, the more exciting it seemed. So, in 2006, we took our first group of ten students to Cape Town, and it was an experience like no other. The group returned full of enthusiasm with so many wonderful stories to share, including how they high-fived Desmond Tutu.

People talk about there being no such thing as coincidences in life, but rather God-incidences, and I'm sure that given my background, us meeting Archbishop Desmond Tutu was one of those such times. It all happened by chance. We were making an educational visit to the cathedral and while we were there I got chatting to some volunteers who asked if we were planning to come to communion with the Archbishop. I hadn't known it was even a possibility, but the guy told me that if we were around for the Friday morning service, then the Archbishop would be there.

Our group of 15-year-olds was aghast at the suggestion of getting up for a 7.30 a.m. communion service, until I explained that Archbishop Desmond Tutu would be there, and they decided that going to church so early might not be such a bad thing after all. 'Wow, if church was like that at home I'd definitely be going,' one of the boys said on the way back. I had to agree with him on the wow factor. It was a special day. When we arrived there were only about thirty or forty other people in the cathedral, and, although no one knew we were coming, during the prayers, because of the diocesan link, the Archbishop prayed for the Diocese of York. At the peace, the Archbishop greeted everyone and asked any guests to stand up and say where they were from. When it came to our turn he was delighted to hear that we were from a school in York, and instead of shaking hands he high-fived all the young people in our group. The kids certainly hadn't been expecting that, or that he would stay around to have his photograph taken with them after the service so that they could come back and share their memories with the rest of the school.

The Archbishop's welcome and hospitality made us all feel really valued that day, but the experience, although incredible, wasn't a one-off. The welcome we received from everyone, and still receive each time we go, knocks me sideways. There is an outpouring of hospitality, warmth, assistance and openness, that I've never experienced anywhere else. At home, one of the biggest challenges when we have visitors is finding someone to put them up, or drive them to the airport, or whatever we need someone to do. That never seems to be a problem in Africa. There you'll have ten people offering to put you up, or if you go to a church service, afterwards someone will invite you to Sunday dinner and someone else will ask if you'd like to come over for a barbecue, or a 'bri' as they call it. I think that the difference in attitude is partly born out of them having to do those things for one another for decades, but it's also largely born out of their faith – living the way the church was living in Acts. Experiencing that warmth first-hand makes me question how I am living out that aspect of my spiritual life, and that aspect of my life in general.

I know the experience has also touched the young people who have travelled with us, in so many different ways. For some, the impact is obvious, particularly from the community work we do. On our first trip we did some work at the Red Cross Children's Hospital. Before going there one of our students was certain that she wanted to pursue an acting career. She is now at university studying medicine, after completely changing the direction of her career path based on what she saw that day.

On another trip the young people worked at an AIDS orphanage in the township of Khayelitsha, which is home to dozens of children from six months of age to eight years old, whose parents have died of AIDS and who are themselves infected by the HIV virus. The pupils painted several large murals in the children's playroom and sleeping areas, and one girl, who had made bracelets initially to fund her own trip, was so moved by what she saw that she kept on making more bracelets when she returned home, sending any money she made back to the orphanage.

On our last couple of trips we've spent time at Sizisa Ukhanyo pre-school in the township of Khayelitsha. When we first visited, the pre-school was housed in a small shack that had originally been built as a polling booth for the 1994 elections. We painted it to help make it look a bit better, but while we were there the teacher in charge told us about some land she had, and how she would love to expand and make the school that little bit bigger.

Today the pre-school has an extra classroom and is fifty per cent bigger because people at Archbishop Holgate's School raised money to make it possible. It was amazing that God delivered the new classroom just as we arrived for our next visit two years later. It meant that we were able to paint the walls, lay the floor tiles, and see what a difference our help has made to the children who go there. It was wonderful to be able to come home and share that news with the rest of the school, to show that by working together as a school community we had created a lasting legacy that is making a difference in the lives of so many young people.

Over the eight years we've been going to South Africa I feel that I've made some real friends and I've seen many other friendships develop and grow. The internet is great for maintaining these friendships. I'll see a young person in school and they'll tell me what someone they met is up to in Cape Town. It kind of makes the planet smaller.

In celebrating helping others the school is celebrating the joy of friendship, and that must surely benefit us in the UK too. Life can be difficult and is a struggle at times, but friends help one another, they do things for one another and don't keep a score of it, because they do it out of love.

In the UK we can be so reticent about talking about what God is doing in our lives, whereas the people I've met in South Africa will speak from the heart about their faith. While I'm not sure that I've got any better at talking about how God has worked in my life, by going to South Africa I've collected a wealth of spiritual anecdotes that have given me a mechanism to speak about what I've seen and how it's impacted on my life. Sometimes, if I get bogged down with the trivial details of work or of interpersonal relationships, I close my eyes and picture the different places I've been to in South Africa and the people I've met there. I'll think about how an issue might feature in their lives and often it gives me the reality check I need to get my priorities right. It makes me realise what really matters in my life, and while we all fail and we all mess up, I think perhaps God is helping me, through my experiences in South Africa, to deal with things at home in the UK a little bit differently.

9 *Regaining Faith*

Izzy McDonald-Booth

Izzy McDonald-Booth is a member of St George's
Church in Jesmond. Although she has always believed
in God, for many years Izzy felt uncomfortable talking
about her faith. Being more open about being a
Christian wasn't easy at first, but it has been
surprisingly positive, deepening and enriching both her
faith and her relationships.

John Sentamu writes:

*Sometimes our lives can feel very lonely places – it can feel like God
is distant and that there is nowhere we can take our doubts and
frustrations. However the reality is, even if we are temporarily
blinded to the fact, God is always right there with us – ready to
support us and listen to our troubles.*

It is good to be honest with God – he knows everything about us and our lives anyway! Our church lives should not be separate from our everyday lives – you cannot hide who you are from God.

God can cope with anything we can throw at him – our pain and passions, our hope and disappointments, the things that hurt us deep inside that no one else can see.

In this chapter, Izzy tells us how her experience of church put her off for many years. Let this story help remind us to listen to others and serve their needs, rather than sitting in judgement.

We need to ensure that church is a welcoming space, a safe place, where people can explore their doubts and frustrations freely with God.

✦

I was quiet about being a Christian for a long time. So much so that my friends think I'm suddenly really involved with the church, when really I'm just being more open about being involved in the church.

For as long as I can remember, I've believed in God. I grew up being part of a church and even in my early teens, when my mother stopped going to church with me, I still went along on a Sunday morning. At the time I don't think that I could have told you why I kept going. I suppose it gave me something that I couldn't quite explain. We lived in a small rural village, so I knew other people in the church, but I didn't go along because I felt particularly close to any of the congregation. Although, I probably wouldn't have said it at the time, I went to church because it gave me some closeness to God.

When I left home and went to college, I was in a completely new place where I didn't know anyone or how much involvement I wanted with the church. I didn't always go to the same church at the same time, but I attended a Sunday service more often than not. I felt quite shy and was trying to feel my way. I liked the fact that I could sneak in, stay for the service and disappear. Looking back on it now, I think, why was I doing that? But, at the time, I needed the sustenance of a service, of a liturgy, of a sermon, of a formalised way of praying. That all suited me, I just didn't want to be involved with the community aspect of it. I was a student, I was enjoying myself and I had other things to do. At the time, I didn't want to talk about my faith to anyone in particular, and I didn't want to get involved in all the extra-curricular activities that happen in church.

Perhaps I could have stayed a quiet member of the congregation quite happily, if it was not that I began to feel increasingly uncomfortable with some of the things I was reading and hearing in the media about the church. At the time I was in my early twenties, I was trying to work out what I wanted in life and figure out where I fitted in it all. I was in a same-sex relationship, but I wasn't confident enough in myself to know if I'd be in a same-sex relationship for the rest of my life. At the same time the church was debating whether or not to allow women priests. To me, it sounded as if there was an awful lot of misogynistic talk coming from members of the church, and a lot of people were pontificating about things that made me feel really uncomfortable. Then on top of the discussions about women priests, there were questions being asked about same-sex relationships and how the church viewed them. Was it ok to be a priest and be in a same-sex relationship, or not?

Around that time I heard a sermon in which the vicar made it quite clear that he thought serving priests should not be in same-sex relationships, not sexual relationships anyway. I felt that if he was saying that about priests then he was saying that being in a same-sex relationship is not behaviour that we should be looking up to, and the inference of that for me was that actually I shouldn't be doing that. I didn't feel ashamed, I just felt really, really sad. It was unspoken in a way. He didn't say that being gay is wrong, but it was what I inferred, because if the church is happy to say someone can't be in a same-sex relationship and be a priest then obviously that has implications for the rest of us, because we like to look up to priests, to seek advice and seek comforting words from them.

I don't know who the vicar was because I wasn't involved enough to know who was giving the sermons, and I certainly wasn't confident enough to make an appointment and have it out with him. Instead, I just stopped going to church. I wasn't angry, I just felt that if I was open at church about what was happening in my life, then I probably wouldn't be welcome. Now I know that probably wasn't the case, that the vicar's sermon was only one person's opinion. Yet, hearing all of that at the time, I thought, well, I still have my personal belief, but what's the point in me coming to sit somewhere where people are so disapproving of the way I'm living my life?

For the next couple of years I didn't go to church. Whatever church had given me before I realised that I needed it, because I missed it. I needed some spiritual sustenance, but without the church I couldn't see where I was going to get it. So, I started to dip my toe in again. I'd pop in to different churches. Sometimes I would go to a prayer service, other times I might go to an Evensong, or if there was a communion service one night in the week I might go along to that. It took me about ten years before I was going back to a regular Sunday service, and for the first three or four years of those I sneaked in the back, as I'd always done, and didn't make any contact with the community there.

Talking about how I felt during that time feels slightly ridiculous to me now. I guess I was listening quietly to what the clergy were saying and the messages were different, they were more inclusive than I had imagined. I suppose I had relaxed more too. I was more comfortable with myself, and felt more able to talk to people at the church, without worrying that I needed to hide who I was. Also, instead of taking the view of one person or one newspaper article I started to do some research myself into what the church's view was on certain subjects and to consider what the church as a larger organisation was doing. I would look up the discussions going on in the House of Bishops and in the House of Lords and find out what senior members of the church had to say. I suppose you could say that I became more switched on about what was actually happening, rather than reacting to a headline or to my own feelings. That shift happened quite gradually but eventually when debates arose in the church I began to see them as that, debates, with more than one side. Now I realise that there will be as many viewpoints as there are people. I may not agree with a viewpoint, but that viewpoint may not necessarily be representative of the church as a whole, and even if the person at the top says something that I don't agree with, then I'm happy to say, well, he's head of the church but he's also human. I can disagree with him and there are probably plenty of other people in the church who disagree too and that's ok. Before, I felt that whatever the head of the church was saying, I had to believe. I viewed the church as much more prescriptive than I do now.

Becoming more informed helped me to be comfortable in my own views. I became aware of organisations within the church, such as Inclusive Church, that were pushing for change and pushing for things to move on in a positive way. It opened my eyes to what was really happening and that made me feel more comfortable about going to worship somewhere on a Sunday. I no longer had to go along and pretend a whole lot of stuff didn't matter, when actually it did. Inclusive church to me means that whatever I decide to do, whatever relationship I decide to have, I'm not going to be rejected, and I'm not going to be frowned upon.

Once I started getting involved in the community of the church I found out about a course on exploring theology. It was one night a week for a year, and I could make a commitment to that. I was interested to learn a bit more about the church, what it was doing and where the ideas were coming from. I was pleased I joined. The group was a mix of people from all denominations, which made for great discussion. Doing the course opened my eyes to the fact that not everybody in the church thinks the same thing. We can have different views, we can have debates and that is perfectly fine.

The course also made me aware of the work that the church does in tackling poverty, both in the UK and overseas. I was overwhelmed by the enormous numbers of Christians who volunteer, and as I result I volunteered to help out at a drop-in centre for asylum seekers. I wanted to put myself to some use and volunteering felt like a good thing to do. I was helping, but I got something back in return that I hadn't expected. Just talking to people about their lives and what they'd been through made me realise that what I sometimes worry about is nothing compared to what other people have to go through, leaving war-torn countries and witnessing torture and killing. It definitely put my life into perspective and I realised how lucky I am.

You could say that now I've got involved in church life, I've really put my oar in. Now I help to teach the Sunday school, I help out with the publicity and the marketing for the church and I'm a member of the Parochial Church Council. How all that fitted with the rest of my life, however, didn't feel straight forward. Almost all my friends outside of church are unbelievers, and because for a long while I hadn't made any proper friends at the church I felt alone in my belief. It was like I was living two separate lives. I was living my normal life, going about my business and seeing friends for coffee and going to work, then on a Sunday I'd have this profound experience in church that would sometimes last all day, but I never talked to anyone about it. I kept my spiritual life and my church life completely separate from everything else about me. That had been ok for a long time, but now it was jarring and I felt lonely.

I made a decision to be more open about my faith. It is not that I ever lied about it, I didn't, but if someone asked what I did on Sunday then I might have told them about the things I did outside of church. So I decided that if it came up in conversation I would tell people about the church things I did as well.

The reality of being open about my faith was very different to how I had imagined it might be. I suppose I was worried about getting a negative reaction, and people dismissing my faith as a load of nonsense. That never happened, not with friends or work colleagues anyway. The only negative experiences I've had have been in relationships where the other person hasn't believed and I've really struggled with that. At one point I was in a relationship where the other person just constantly wanted to have discussions about if God exists and why. I just found it really wearing after a while.

More than anything, I'd say the reaction I've had to sharing my faith has been positive. I've been surprised at the conversations my faith has opened and how people will tell me about things in their lives that they might not have done before. Some people ask if they could come to my church, other people want to talk about their belief or their struggle with belief. I've been asked to say prayers for people, or to remember people in certain ways. It wasn't what I expected at all, but I'm aware that with that openness comes a responsibility. I don't take that with a heavy heart, but it's just an awareness. I'm more aware of how I behave and what I say. If something is happening that I don't agree with I'm more vocal about it than I might have been before.

I once heard someone say, you're the only Bible that some people have read. That stuck with me. For people who don't attend church, they might have some belief, they might not, but if I'm the only person they know who is a Christian then their view of Christianity is me.

I don't always talk about church or my faith, but I don't try to hide it either. My belief is intrinsic to who I am, it affects the way that I view the world and the way that I experience the world. It is central to everything and in a way it always has been. The difference now is that I'm more open about it and the change has definitely enriched my life.

10 Being Called to Be the Best

Andy Grant

The Revd Andy Grant is a curate in Boston Spa.
Before being ordained, Andy served in HM Forces in
1st Battalion the Royal Gloucestershire, Berkshire and
Wiltshire Regiment, until a life-threatening accident
caused him to rethink his faith and his vocation.

John Sentamu writes:

*I always say that our British armed forces are the best of the best.
They do a difficult job in impossible situations, putting themselves
in the line of fire to protect others. Every morning I pray for our
forces serving overseas and for the families left behind.*

*Our brave soldiers, air personnel and naval forces make incred-
ible sacrifices for our Queen and country. Our freedoms are built
on democracy, openness and peace. Sadly the same cannot be said
for every country around the globe.*

Often our forces are called to be the peacemakers on behalf of the global community through the United Nations; it is an important but unenviable task. Loving your neighbour sometimes means that you have to protect them too.

But what does it really mean to be the best we can be?

This chapter looks at the story of Andy, a former soldier who suffered a life-threatening accident in the line of duty – and who ended up becoming a priest. He explains how his personal experience of the army forced him to re-evaluate God's purpose in his own life.

⁂

I never thought much about death when I joined the army in my late teens. Although being a soldier meant that I might lose my life in conflict, it never crossed my mind as a real possibility. Everything about the job was exciting and going on tour was one big adventure. I felt immortal. Nothing could touch me.

Then, while serving in the Balkans, I was involved in a terrible accident. For the first time in my army career I feared for my life, and it changed my perspective on everything.

The day it happened I was serving as Lance Corporal with the former Royal Gloucestershire, Berkshire and Wiltshire Regiment. Conflict had broken out in what was then Yugoslavia and the United Nations had enlisted troops to patrol a safe haven in Gorazde. We had just finished a patrol and were returning to our base when the Saxon vehicle we were travelling in started to tip. This was an armoured personnel carrier, built to be driven across rough terrain and through water up to 90cm deep. Although we were driving down a steep valley, when it is at an angle like that you know something is very wrong. I was in the turret behind the commander who started screaming down the radio to the driver to find out what had happened. If a vehicle like that rolls when you're half way out, that's it – game over.

The driver was killed in the accident, so we'll never know exactly what happened or why the vehicle went out of control. It all happened so fast that I had no sense of being in control or thinking to myself, 'I'd better duck'. I was probably in shock, but I felt a force either push me under or pull me down. It definitely wasn't one of the other guys grabbing and pulling me, I know that. As my body was thrown against the metal interior I looked over and saw one of my colleagues. My face was the last thing he remembers seeing before he lost consciousness, as the vehicle rolled over an edge and bounced. It wasn't a straight drop, but it was very steep. There was a sense of us rotating through the air and then crashing against the undergrowth. Everything inside – the kit, ammunition boxes and vehicle batteries, it all loosened up and was rattling around me. No one could survive this, I was sure of that. I thought about my family momentarily, then I was just waiting for it – the big whack on the head and the darkness to fall.

I was certain I would die. Then the vehicle landed on its side momentarily, a small door opened, I fell through it, the vehicle lifted off me and continued its descent down the hill leaving me sitting on the hillside. I looked down. My body armour, helmet and webbing had all been ripped off and I was left wearing only my boots and uniform. I didn't know how I'd got undressed or where my kit was, but my arms and legs were all there and working. I couldn't believe it. I was alive. There was nothing to say through my tears except, 'Thank you, Jesus!'

I never expected anyone to come out of that vehicle alive, but I soon realised that I wasn't the only survivor, hearing another of our men cry out. Crawling a few feet to reach him I saw he was badly injured so I stayed with him on the hillside until some Bosniak soldiers came out of their positions to help us down the tracks to the bottom of the valley. When we eventually arrived back in camp we learned that three of our men had been killed and we were two of five survivors. We were all taken on to hospital. I had damage to my left thigh and my elbow, ligament damage to my knees and there was an open wound on my face which needed stitching. However, compared to some of the others my injuries were light.

I know that nothing I did saved my life that day. I was utterly in the hands of God, or chance, or whatever you want to call it. I couldn't have prepared for it. No amount of training could have taught me what to do if the vehicle I was travelling in tumbled a thousand feet down the side of a valley. It was very frightening and took a great presence of mind to stay calm. Yet somehow I did manage to stay calm. Obviously I was in shock, but I was calm, because when I was carried to the bottom of the valley I felt ok. Deep inside, I knew I was ok.

After the accident I came home to get patched up properly. I needed a couple of operations and time to heal. While recovering I was probably quite unpleasant to live with. My body was full of adrenaline, drive and energy, yet at the same time it was trying to repair itself, which meant that I wasn't able to do lots of things that I felt I should be able to. As soon as I was fit enough I wanted to be back on tour.

If I'm honest I wasn't completely better when I decided to return to the Balkans. My knees were still in pain, but I didn't give much thought to how physically demanding the job would be. I just pulled on my backpack and away I went. The idea of being back on tour was exciting and it felt the right thing to do. That feeling didn't last long. On the flight over I began to have second thoughts. By the time we landed, all the desire and motivation I had for the trip had gone. If I could have got on a plane home a minute later I would have done. I asked for a private word with my platoon commander, 'You've got to get me on the first plane out of here. I can't stay.'

'I can't get you out of here now,' he told me, 'but when the tour finishes I'll make sure you're on the first flight.'

True to his word I was on an early flight home, but not until I'd first served another seven weeks. To add to my woes, it was mid-winter and the weather was a real challenge. I'd go to sleep cold and wake up even colder. Trying to function and exist in such extreme temperatures was difficult enough, without having a job to do. Out on the hills my shaving foam and toothpaste froze making it an effort simply to stay clean and in a fit state. Far from being exciting, the days were a long hard slog, but the toughest part of all was getting back into a Saxon vehicle.

Patrolling vehicles through Gorazde was like driving through hell. The nearest thing I could relate it to was looking at footage of World War II. The place wasn't totally annihilated, but the area had been shelled, children ran around in bare feet, homes had no windows, roofs were missing and there was no electricity or power of any kind. It was a place with its soul ripped out, and there we were, in our blue berets, trying our best to support and protect the desperate people still living there.

It is easy to look at a place of great darkness and oppression and think, where is God in all of this mess? Part of my brain thought that too. At the same time, in the midst of all that upset, I knew that God was there. It was almost because I felt frightened of being there, that I couldn't just accept the horror of it all, that I knew God was there. I couldn't push him away. I sensed his comfort. I knew he wanted something better for this land and for these people than this. Without God it would have felt completely meaningless and I probably would have been in hell – or at least hell of some description.

The war in Bosnia lasted three years, nine months, one week and six days. It ended on 14 December 1995 and I left in April of that year. The accident and my time there had a profound effect on me and how I viewed my life. I started to think in much greater depth than I'd ever done before about my life, about God and about the time I spent with my wife and children. In many ways it kick-started my faith, which had become a bit staid, and I began to attend church on a much more regular basis.

After leaving Bosnia, the whole regiment, families and all, flew to Cyprus. We stayed in Cyprus for two years, during which time I began attending a Church of England chapel. I started taking my faith a lot more seriously and, on returning to England in 1997, I decided to get confirmed.

A short while after my confirmation an incumbent at the church pulled me to one side and said: 'I'd like you to consider exploring a vocation.' The idea sounded very nice, but at the same time I thought it odd, bearing in mind that I was from the infantry. However, something he said must have stuck with me because I ticked along with the idea for a little bit. Then, about a year later my love for being an infantry soldier just died and was replaced with a real desire to work in army administration as a clerk. So, after ten tears as a soldier I processed a transfer and within the next six months had completed two clerk training courses, a promotion course and a tour of South Armagh.

No sooner had I started work as a clerk, than I found out that the army had a welfare service and decided I wanted to work there. To do that I'd need to be promoted to sergeant, get a recommendation and do further training. It seemed a tall order at the time, but I went for it anyway, and, after three or four years as a clerk, I got in, spending the next seven years in occupational welfare. Looking back, I can see the skills I learned in those jobs as foundational building blocks leading me to where I am now. It was great experience for pastoral work, and meant that my move from the army into the church was not really so much of a leap as a next step.

A week after my ordination I found myself back in Gorazde, this time as a minister, leading a service to re-dedicate some memorial stones to my three colleagues, Privates Phillip Armstrong, Martin Dowdell, and Chris Turner, who died in the accident, and Private Ben Hinton, who died in a separate accident four days earlier. After their deaths, two memorials were carved in marble by a Bosnian refugee and placed where they died. However, at the end of the British mission in Bosnia and Herzegovina in 2007, and in accordance with Army policy, the memorials were removed and held in storage at the Regimental Office in Gloucester.

Colonel Ian Harris, my commander at the time, had the idea of getting the stones back into their rightful place, so a few of us raised funds to get the stones cleaned up and back out there.

Returning to the site of the accident with ex-soldiers, guys I hadn't seen for years, brought it all back to me. The accident itself was extremely traumatic and I recall God's protecting hand on my life that day in a very real way. What is difficult to understand or explain is why those other lads were not saved too? It is a question that will never be answered in this lifetime.

My life as a curate is very different to that of a soldier, but part of me hasn't changed. I never had a problem with being a soldier and to this day I still support the forces. I'm more aware than I was as a teenager that conflict and warfare creates a huge amount of suffering, but I hold on to the theology that chaplains promote in the army, that to love your neighbour sometimes means that you need to protect your neighbour. As long as the army is fulfilling that role – behaving itself as it were, abiding by the Geneva Convention, using minimum force and protecting life where necessary – then I'm happy to support it.

The guys I met up with again, they all knew that. They all knew that I'd followed this vocation to be a priest, but they didn't treat me any differently. They were pulling my leg all over the place, like they used to in the old days, and I really liked that. They all knew that I went to church when I was a soldier. I could still be myself and they respected the fact that I am still the Andy they know and I am a priest as well. In some ways it is more of a surprise for me than it is to them, for although I hadn't seen it in myself at the time, for them my vocation was inevitable. 'Glad you made it, Andy,' they smiled. 'We always knew this would happen.'

11   *Wrestling with God*

Sam Foster

Sam Foster is Fresh Expression pioneer minister in Scarborough Deanery, working with traditional churches as well as leading mission initiatives on the street and beach. She was ordained at the age of 23, and at the time was the youngest woman to become an Anglican priest.

John Sentamu writes:

Do you ever make a promise with God? 'Send me anywhere, Lord, but not there.' 'Ask me to do anything, Lord, but not that.' It's often a natural reaction to our own insecurities and fears.

Maybe we worry that we won't have the inner strength to deliver what might be expected of us – but with God, anything is possible.

Do you remember the story of Jonah? God told him to go and preach at Nineveh, to tell people to change their ways. Did Jonah go? No, he jumped on a boat and headed as far away as possible in the opposite direction. He couldn't escape though, and eventually (via the stomach of a giant fish) he ended up back at Nineveh – and saving the lives of thousands.

God is a miracle worker, but he has total faith in us – all we need to do is put our trust in him.

This chapter tells the story of Sam, an inspirational young woman, who couldn't escape God's call to become ordained and serve others.

❖

Next year it will be ten years since I was ordained a priest in the Anglican Church. It's been quite a journey, especially when you think that ten years before I was ordained, just the idea of going into a church had me running in the opposite direction.

At the age of thirteen, church was the last thing on my mind. My mum went to church every Sunday, but apart from going along with her for the odd Christmas service, I wasn't interested. I was too busy hanging out with my friends, playing daft pranks and being the teenage rebel. The issue of women's ordination was in the news, but I never thought about it. The only woman I knew in the church was in *The Vicar of Dibley* on TV.

When I turned fourteen, the topic of confirmation came up in my house. My two sisters had been confirmed at the same age and my mum asked if I would come along to a meeting and consider it. I said, yes, but I only agreed because I love my mum and wanted to please her. I made it quite clear that I would go to church the once and that was it.

The night before we were due to go, I couldn't sleep. I was so anxious, heaven knows what I thought was going to happen to me. When we arrived at the church the next morning, I looked over my shoulder to check that no one could see me going in.

As I walked through the door it was just as I'd expected in one sense, there were predominantly elderly people in the pews and we sang traditional hymns. Then as I listened to the readings they seemed to speak to me in a way that made God feel real. I knew he was real, because I had always believed in my own way, but this felt different. It felt nice and special. The only way I can describe it is the feeling you get when you've been away for a long time and you come back home. It was that same, relieved feeling of being back where you belong.

After the service I said to my mum, 'I'd like to go again.' Soon after that, I couldn't get enough of it and started attending midweek services as well. Basically, I was going as often as I could, until after a few months my mum said to me: 'Well, you can go, but the thing is, I was only wanting to go once a week, not every day.'

I knew then that I wasn't just going to church in order to please my mum. I was going because I wanted to, and from then on I became more and more involved in church life. Looking back, I think it was all a part of my calling to the priesthood, but that wasn't something I could articulate at the time. I was just learning about what it means to be a Christian. Before, I'd thought of the Gospel as a nice story to tell, now it was alive to me. I realised that Christianity isn't about knowledge or following a set of rules. It is a way of life. It can transform how you live and how you impact on other people.

I didn't need to be told this. It wasn't about theorising. I could see the change in my own life. Instead of hanging around with friends and getting up to mischievous things, I became more involved with the church, serving at the altar, teaching Sunday school and helping at the crèche. As the token young person at our church, the vicar asked if I would help set up a youth group. At the time I was living on the Grove Hill estate in Middlesbrough where life for many young people was about sniffing glue, twocking cars and burning them out. That was just how life was. Of course that doesn't mean that everyone who lived there was like that, but in many ways it was a reality that couldn't be escaped.

Naturally, this behaviour worried some of the parents on the estate, who didn't want their sons to end up on the wrong path. So, when I mentioned the youth group they were happy to volunteer as supervisors. They brought their sons along, then their sons brought their mates. I asked my friends to come along too, and the youth group grew from there.

The church was St Oswalds, so we called the group, Ossies. I ended up leading it, and helping to organise lock-ins and sleep-overs in the church building. One night we all sat in a circle and I asked everyone to say one good thing about the person next to them. It was normal for me and my friends to say things like that to each other, but I soon realised that for a lot of the lads in the group, it was the first time they had heard a compliment from anyone. It was clearly embarrassing for some, but once they got over the initial discomfort so many of them said, 'Nobody's ever told me that before', and those feelings bonded us together as a group.

Soon we had loads of young people coming along to the youth group whom we never saw at a Sunday morning service. I don't think that mattered, because through the group God was touching their lives, even if the result wasn't always something to brag about. During the time we ran the youth group, the church was never once vandalised. The vicar's car did get broken into, with the home communion box in the boot. I mentioned this in passing to one of the lads at about ten o'clock in the morning, and by one o'clock that day, although the car didn't reappear, the communion kit was left intact on the doorstep of the vicarage.

It was good to see God working in people's lives. In my own life I wasn't sure what God was calling me to do, and I didn't really want to talk about it to anyone. When these thoughts of ordination would come into my head I would try to negotiate with God, praying, if I do this in church, will you leave me alone? Young people didn't get feelings like this, I was sure of it. Perhaps I was having a nervous breakdown, that was all I could think it could be, so I didn't tell anyone.

We got a new vicar at the parish, who was a woman. She was easy to talk to, and although I thought I was keeping my secret well hidden, she soon saw a pattern to my negotiations. Every six weeks or so I'd be knocking on her door offering to do something else. One week it would be, I think God's calling me to lead Sunday school, and the next I'd say, I think God's calling me to be a reader. This went on until one day she sat down with a big sigh and said, 'How do you know God's not calling you to ordained ministry?'

'Well he is, but this is an easier option,' I admitted. I don't know where the words came from but it was such a relief to let go of this secret I'd been hiding for so long. When I finally did share my feelings with family and friends they said things like, 'Oh well, it was only a matter of time really wasn't it? We're not surprised.' They had no idea how long I'd waited to pluck up the courage to tell them. It was as though while God was getting me ready, he had prepared my family and friends for it as well.

From that moment I felt like doors opened for me and with my vicar's help I started to explore the possibility of ordination. At the time I was nineteen years old and had just finished the first year of my degree in primary education. It was good to be open about my thoughts of ordination, but part of me wanted to stick to my degree so that I couldn't let God in with these other ideas. I suppose that I was still looking for a way out in many ways.

I still wasn't sure that ordination was for me. I started attending Fellowship of Vocation meetings, but there weren't many younger people and while the older people were lovely, I just couldn't relate to them.

When it came for me to have an interview with the bishop, I was relieved to hear that he had been against the ordination of women. I thought, great, that means he'll say no, and I can get on with my life. As it turned out we had a lovely meeting. I think that was partly because I wasn't trying to gain approval, I'd already convinced myself that he'd say no and I could move on.

Then, as I left his house, the bishop said, 'Right, I'm going to write a report and I'm going to tell you then what my recommendation is.'

Yeah, good, get on with it, I thought.

'I'll tell you now, I'm going to recommend you without any exception.'

Whoops, that messed up my plans. The bishop's response was completely unexpected, but, as I walked down the path from his house something in me changed. I decided I would test this vocation. This path was the way for me now and I was happy to see what it would bring.

At the selection conference I really wanted to be chosen. Of course, that still didn't stop me wondering, what am I doing here? I still wasn't sure how it had happened, but I knew it was an amazing privilege. Sure, I felt I didn't fit, that never changed, but I did hope that I would be selected.

Although I do feel very much a part of the church, you could say in one sense that I am still coming at it from the outside. In Scarborough, where I work now, I'm known as the vicar without a church. I'm a Fresh Expressions pioneer vicar and, although I work with all twenty-seven Anglican churches in the deanery, a large part of my job is meeting people where they are, rather than expecting them to come into church.

I work with a team and one of the things we do is sacred space on the beach. We run it during the summer months where we invite people to light candles in memory of a loved one, or a troubled situation or to give thanks for something. Some of the people who pass by have got very little idea about Christianity, let alone church, but because they are remembering someone or something close to them and it's on the beach, they are really taken with the idea. We're not there Bible bashing or collecting money, we are simply offering care and compassion to people, and it is appreciated. We are always thanked for being there. We've been running it for four years now with an ecumenical team. Some people want prayer, some people want to talk, and other people just want to be in the space, or write a name in the sand, or take a photograph. Being there has been described like walking into a bubble and coming out feeling different, feeling hope. To hear people talk about something changing within them is amazing. Who knows where their searching will end?

I still have family in Middlesbrough and when I'm visiting I'll sometimes bump into lads from my youth group days. Some of them have got children of their own now, but they'll always stop me and say, 'I remember Ossie's nights and what we used to do with you. It was brill.' That's really nice to hear, because I didn't just wake up one morning in my early twenties and think, I want to be a vicar. I can think of easier things to do, but God's put me here and now I can't imagine doing anything else. Although I was young to be ordained, I signed up for life, and I always say, even if I was stacking shelves in a supermarket I'd still be pioneering.

12   Serving the Marginalised

Rodney Marshall

Father Rodney Marshall is Vicar of St Helen's Athersley in the Wakefield Diocese. He founded the Romero Project in 2004, which provides a safety net for those who find themselves marginalised by society. Run from a centre attached to the church, the project employs two members of staff and has a team of volunteers, many of whom have been helped out of a personal crisis by the Romero Project in the past.

John Sentamu writes:

Oscar Romero, a Catholic priest in poverty-stricken El Salvador, once said: 'When I fed the people they called me a saint. When I asked why the people were hungry, they called me a Communist.'

As Christians we should be ready to speak truth into difficult situations. Let us have the courage to say how things are, rather than feel we have to pussyfoot around challenges that lie before us.

Prevarication gets us nowhere when practical action is required.

One of the great things about the Catholic movement both in England and throughout the world is its concern with living the social Gospel. Throughout history, priests and parishioners have often found themselves working in areas of severe inequality. Areas where there are high unemployment rates, low job opportunities, poor health and education, and an overall feeling of worthlessness amongst the people who live there. We are called to demand better. We are called to demand justice.

For Oscar Romero, his own brave stand cost him his life. The cross that I wear today was given to me by a young survivor of the El Salvadorean civil war – the words of Romero are on the back: 'Peace will flower when Love and Justice pervade our environment.'

We would do well to remember that the Church is not the building in which we worship, it is the people who put God's love into action. He calls us not to serve those inside the congregation, but those outside and on the periphery of society.

Let us consider how we can use our church buildings better, and how we can ensure our sacred spaces serve the whole community.

This chapter tells the story of Rodney, a vicar who founded a project serving those marginalised within his community, offering hope where there is despair. He called the project 'The Oscar Romero Centre'.

I'm a priest, not a social worker. My job is to care for souls, but what is the use in saying to folk whose lives are in a mess, 'God loves you, get on with it'?

I know, because I've been there myself. I remember as a child being told by my mother to be very, very quiet because the rent man was coming. We had to hide until he had gone because we didn't have the money to pay him. Although I wasn't aware of it as such at the time, we lived in poverty. I grew up in the Moss Side area of Manchester just after the war, where I experienced first-hand how money worries, debt and housing problems can prevent people from being all that God created them to be. Jesus said that he came so that people would have life and have it in all its fullness. In my view, that means that my job is not simply about preparing people for the life to come, it is about caring for them in the here and now. It is about helping people live the fullest life that they can, and they can't do that when they're fighting against poverty all the time.

I'm not a bleeding-heart liberal. I don't just feel sorry for people. Patronisation has become a disease. I don't make an effort to get alongside the people in my community, because I am already alongside them. I don't see a difference between us – people are people. Most of my ministry has been spent on housing estates or in pit villages. It's all much of a muchness really. Where I live now might not be the inner city I grew up in, but many of the struggles are the same, and, on a practical level, I can understand them because I've been there. I'm not different from these people at all. Just because I've been ordained doesn't take away that part of who I am, and there is a kind of solidarity in that.

I've been Vicar of St Helen's in Athersley for fifteen years now. The parish sits in the middle of three large council estates on the edge of Barnsley and according to statistics from the Church Urban Fund, which helps tackle poverty in England, we are one of the most deprived parishes in the country. Not long after I arrived, the then Bishop of Wakefield, Nigel McCulloch, set off on a great trail, visiting every parish in the diocese. The poor man must have eaten pork pies and sausage rolls ten times a week for a year on his travels, and in return he set us all a challenge – to get involved in the local community. In other words, how could we show God's love to people where we lived?

The Bishop's challenge spoke to me at the core of my faith – the doctrine of the incarnation underpinned everything that I did, from celebrating the sacraments to dealing with people. Yet, there were still the questions of what to do and how to do it? I didn't need a deprivation measure to tell me that there was unmet need in my parish. I saw it every day, at funerals, weddings, baptisms, and on my normal pastoral round. If it was the church's job, as I believed it was, to incarnate God's love into the community, then we had to show that love in a way that mattered, in a way that would help people to live fuller lives. It was out of that idea that the Romero Project was born, named after Oscar Romero, a former Archbishop of El Salvador who was assassinated in 1980 during the country's civil war. A martyr in my lifetime, Oscar Romero was a champion of the poor, eventually paying the ultimate price for speaking out against the government on equality and justice. His motto was, 'Don't aspire to have more, but to be more.' I liked that too, because his fight wasn't about money, it was about social injustice. Money is vital to life, whether we like it or not. That doesn't mean that we should aspire to have more material things, but there is a level of money needed to lift people out of poverty, to allow them to think about other things in life and begin to follow their dreams.

I realise that in Athersley we weren't in a situation like the civil war in El Salvador, but the essence of what we were trying to achieve with our project was the same – we were trying to stand up for people who were marginalised and poor, to give a voice to those in society whose cries for help were not being heard. Sometimes that could mean us speaking out against the government as well.

I've often heard it said that priests should stick to religion and not get involved in politics. Party politics, maybe – I don't see it is as my job to support one particular party over another. However, politics in the general sense is another matter. It is about the way we organise our society, and the Gospel has something to say about that. It speaks about how we should organise our society in a fair and just way. If we believe that God became man in Jesus, which as Christians we do, then we believe that every human being has a worth and a value that no one can take away from them, by virtue of the fact that they've been created as children of God. So, if you have politicians who are putting forward policies that are not going to enable people to live in a way that values their worth as human beings then I think that the church has got not only a right, but a moral duty to speak out. Blow whether people like it or don't like it, that's neither here nor there. Whether they listen or not is another matter.

In this sense it is impossible to separate politics and religion. Jesus didn't, so I don't suppose I can either, although it does get me into a little bit of hot water occasionally. During the Miners' Strike I was fairly active in the village where I lived and used to go picketing. To me, this was what the people I had the cure of souls of were doing and therefore I should stand alongside them. Not everyone liked that, obviously. However, the older I get, the less bothered I am about what I say and about what other people might think of it.

It was with that attitude, the desire to give a voice to those who didn't have one, that our project took shape. The idea was to create a place in the community where anyone could come and get advice on issues that were preventing them from living a full life. Often that was attached to a lack of money, but not always. It could be a need for friendship, community, family members, or the need to deal with something that had been impacting on a person since childhood. We wanted to be able to help with all of these problems in an environment that was safe, friendly, impartial and free.

Of course, we're not miracle workers. To achieve all of this would take more than a couple of people who wanted to change the world. So, we set about building relationships with other organisations, such as the Citizens Advice Bureau, Connexions and Alcoholics Anonymous, which enabled us to bring in the necessary expertise without recreating it. In essence, we hoped to provide a trusted ear and a bridge to introduce people to organisations and groups who may be able to help them.

We set up a centre by converting some space that wasn't being used at the back of the church. Basically, we got some money and had a big wall built across to create a separate space, which had its own entrance, an office, a kitchen and a small room where people could talk in private. We opened our doors and people came in more numbers than we could have imagined – people whose lives were made very difficult by the circumstances in which they found themselves.

Now, obviously we weren't going to help people change their lives overnight. If we'd thought that then we'd be a bit disillu-sioned. Sometimes the story that someone comes with is so complex that it needs to be unpicked over time. What we can do is to listen and give people time to get to the crux of what it is that has led them to the situation in which they find themselves.

When people come with a crisis it is important to help them to get out of that crisis, but that is not where our work stops. Usually when you give people time to talk things through they will mention other things in their lives that are positive, even if they've lost sight of that fact. It's nice to help to pull those things out and to see someone focus on the positive things in their life. So often people will say, 'When I get out of this mess I'm going to do ...', and I'll say, 'What's stopping you doing that now?' I don't think that most people who come to the centre for help will ever have a lot more, but they can be more. Most people have dreams, whatever they may be. Part of our job is about encouraging people to focus on what they can do, rather than what they can't, to think about what steps they can take, however small those steps may be.

Of course, we're not stupid, in so far as we realise that there are some people who come through the doors who are taking the proverbial by trying to pull the wool over our eyes. But even people like that deserve our help, they deserve to be heard too. I always think that if you've got a system that is so tight that it can't be abused in some way then it's too tight and the people who need it will miss out. So, I'm quite happy to put up with having someone come in and try to con me occasionally for the sake of the fact that the vast majority of people do get the genuine help that they need.

There is much genuine help needed and we see that every day. In just two hours this morning at the centre we had someone from the National Careers Service helping people write a CV and look for job opportunities; a local volunteer helping another local resident repair his laptop; a young woman who only speaks Mandarin and needed help translating; a woman who was desperate after receiving a letter about her son's disability living allowance being stopped, and another woman in the private room who needed a crisis loan.

At first, some people were a bit iffy about the project being connected to the church and thought that it was just a ruse to get them through the door, but we've been here for eight years now and people realise that it's not like that. The work we do is unconditional. One or two people who use the centre have started coming to church, but nobody pushed them into it or even asked them, probably, they just came.

Often I'll hear people say, 'Isn't it marvellous that church does something like this for people like me – I don't even go to church.' Recently, one of the members of an Alcoholics Anonymous group that meets in the centre said to me, 'I don't go to church, but I like it that we meet here. The fact that we are in one part and people are praying in another part of the building, well I think somehow or other that is good for our meeting.' He couldn't explain why he thought that, other than he did seem to feel that the church bit mattered. I don't know if I can explain either, except that even for people who don't attend services, through the Romero Project they see the church as being part of their lives and an important part of the community.

13   A Modern-Day Christian

Malc Clark

Malc Clark is the Key Stage 3 co-ordinator and music ministry co-ordinator for the York Schools and Youth Trust (YoYo). Founded in 1996, YoYo is a non-denominational charity, which works in schools across York to communicate the Christian faith. Malc also sings and plays guitar in a four-piece rock band, This Resistance, whose music is inspired by his faith.

John Sentamu writes:

If I asked you to describe someone who was a missionary, how would you reply?

Maybe you would instantly think of a man in a white linen suit, wearing a panama hat, walking around a distant part of Africa?

I imagine most people would probably picture someone boarding a boat or plane heading to a far-off land from where they would not return for a very long time. But actually that isn't necessarily what mission is all about.

Mission should begin right here. There is no better place to start reaching out to those in need with a message of hope than in the communities in which we live. Whilst I thank God for those who have bravely taken the Gospel to other countries, you don't need to travel to a faraway land when there is real need for hope and transformation on our doorstep.

So what does it really mean to be a missionary in the modern world? It's about using our skills, talents and experience to serve others. It's about having a heart for change. It's about showing love and care where it is currently absent. Being a missionary is not a holiday, it's a calling.

And what does the modern missionary look like? You can answer that question by simply picking up a mirror – the modern missionary looks like you and me.

This chapter looks at the story of Malc, someone who was called to be a missionary working with young people in Yorkshire.

I really enjoy talking about my faith to other people, but it's not always easy, especially when I'm being grilled by 16-year-olds on a tricky subject. I'm often asked why I believe in God? Or, I get questions about lifestyle choices, such as drinking and sex. They are big questions with no right or wrong answers. Rather, the answers we give reflect the way we choose to live. When teenagers ask me these questions it is generally because they are trying to work out their own place in the world and what they think about God and about life. We may not always agree, but usually I find that they ask me because they are genuinely interested in my views as a Christian and in how my beliefs influence how I perceive certain issues and how I behave. Talking about these topics helps me too. It helps me to be open to other points of view and to think more clearly about why I believe what I believe. I might believe in God for a very good reason, but, doing the job I do, I need to be able to explain that to others. It's a great privilege to be able to share views and listen to other opinions. Without getting too heavy, we are lucky to have freedom of speech in our country, and it shouldn't be taken for granted.

I haven't always found expressing myself easy. When I was younger, I would never be the one to stand up and talk in front of people. I was always too nervous to do anything like that. Through my involvement in youth ministry, I've certainly found myself growing in ways that I never expected.

My parents are Christians and I would always have said that I was a Christian, but it took me a long time for me to understand what that meant. When I was sixteen I really began to question my faith. Why did I believe what I believed? Did I even believe it? Did I want to believe it?

Like most teenagers at that age I had a lot of other things going on in my life and around in my head. I was trying to figure out who I was and where I was going. How my faith fitted into my life and how I related to God, if indeed I did, was part of that. I wanted to think for myself and decide for myself, so I got a Bible and started reading. I opened the New Testament and started reading the book, Paul's letter to the Philippians. It was written by the apostle Paul while he was in prison, yet it is full of joy and confidence. The more I read, the more I became aware of my need for a saviour and to be forgiven. That summer holiday, between leaving school and going to college, I decided that I wanted to be a Christian.

I'd chosen the Sixth Form I was going to because it had a good music course, but I didn't know many people at all. I didn't go in all guns blazing, telling people I was a Christian, but I was really looking forward to living out my faith and was excited about sharing it with other people. I set up a Christian Union at the Sixth Form College and began to get more involved with my church. It was through the Christian Union that I became involved with YoYo, a Christian youth charity based in York. Staff and volunteers for YoYo visit different schools teaching about the Christian faith by taking RE lessons and assemblies or running lunchtime and after-school clubs. When YoYo heard about the Christian Union I'd started one of the team began coming along to help out. It was a great encouragement to me and to the group.

All through sixth form I wasn't sure what my next move was going to be. The girl who came from YoYo to support the Christian Union suggested: 'Why don't you get involved in YoYo one day?' At the time I thought that's not my thing. I'm going to go on to Music College. Music was always what I enjoyed doing best and was the main reason I chose the college I did.

I applied to Music College and was offered a place at Leeds. Then through prayer I began to think that maybe that wasn't the right choice for me. I had a strong feeling that God wanted me to work in ministry or missionary work in a full-time capacity. So, I prayed about it some more and started to think about what that might mean for my life.

My first thought was that I would need to hop on a plane or a boat and get involved in an overseas mission. I read up about different missionary organisations, what they did, where they worked, and was seriously considering joining one as my next step. As part of my preparation I attended a service about missionary work and ministry. The preacher said: 'For many of you, when you think you're called to missionary work, you will think that means you've got to get in a boat and sail off somewhere across the world.'

I was listening thinking, 'Yeah, that's me. That's exactly what I think.'

Then he added: 'That's not how it should be. You start at home, you start where you're at.'

The preacher's words posed a real challenge to me. When he'd started speaking I thought that he was going to affirm everything I'd been planning in my mind up until that point, and now I just felt confused. The first thing that came into my mind was YoYo. It was the summer holidays so, being away from the Christian Union, I hadn't thought about YoYo for a good month or two. Unsure of what to do, I prayed a very simple prayer:

'Lord, if you want me to work for YoYo and give some time to that work, please make it clear to me within a week, otherwise I'm going to send this application form off to the missionary organisation.'

It's very seldom that coincidences like this happen to me, but the very next morning I woke up to a text from the girl I knew from YoYo. 'Hey, Malc,' she wrote. 'Have you thought any more about getting involved in YoYo?'

I took that message as a clear sign from God that that was what he wanted me to do. I volunteered for a year, thinking that I would do something else after that, but then they offered me a job and I've stayed ever since.

The only down side to missionary work, if you can call it a down side, is in terms of the pay – you certainly wouldn't go into it for the money. If I want to get my own home then I'm going to have to look for other work alongside it. I don't know where I'll end up, but I do see myself using my gifts and the skills I've used at YoYo in the future. Even if I get another job that isn't strictly a youth ministry role, I don't see that as leaving ministry. As a Christian, whatever I'm doing I want to be living out my faith. I don't want to feel that I'm living as two different people, just because I might have two jobs.

When I was doing my gap year at YoYo, to fund that I worked part-time at a supermarket. It was interesting how some people viewed me because I had a faith. Some people assumed I was Jewish, and others thought that because I did some youth ministry work that I must be a religious fanatic. But over time, as I got to know people, they could see that I was up for a laugh and wasn't any different to anyone else. I think that Christians working in an office space or wherever have got a much harder job than someone like myself who is privileged to be working with other Christians and sharing my faith as part of what I do every day. Often Christians in the workplace can be on their own in their beliefs.

There can be a stereotype of Christians as high and mighty, that they think they are really good people who try to be good all of the time. If you tell people that you are a Christian at work, some colleagues will be watching to see if you are living life as you believe, when really there's no difference between a Christian and a non-Christian in terms of their sin and mistakes. Christians mess up too sometimes and it is good to be honest about that, so you don't come across as thinking you're above someone else, that you're taking the moral high ground all the time. It was good for me to build good relationships with people and for them to know that I am a Christian. I didn't need to compromise my beliefs. I wasn't going to go out to get drunk and all that stuff, but I'd still hang out and find other things to do with them and have a good time.

Many people will claim that they don't put people into stereotypes, but when you break a stereotype, they still act surprised. I sing and play guitar in a rock band called This Resistance. It's me and three friends who are also Christians. People are often surprised when they find out that we're Christians. We have no problem witnessing through our lyrics and through what we say on stage, but obviously we don't go on stage and say, 'Hey, we're Christians!'

The band is about the music. We are Christians, we have a faith and love to share that in everything we do, but that doesn't mean that our band is a Christian band. We don't only play for Christians. We do play in schools and at youth events because it is nice to be involved in reaching out with our faith in different ways, building relationships and bridging gaps that sometimes the traditional church can't. We also get invited to play gigs on the secular music scene, which we really enjoy too.

We don't always sing about God or share our faith on stage, but we don't hide it either. We pray before everything we do, down to what sort of guitar we are going to buy. I know that might sound funny, but we prayed about the guitar because it cost a lot of money and we want God to be at the centre of everything we do. That means, our songwriting sessions, the way we perform, and even the relationship we have with the sound guy on a gig, we want God to be a part of it all. For me, God is in everything that I do. I'm just trying to live as a

Christian in the modern day and I hope that by doing that, people will see something in me that they desire for themselves, and that something is God.

14   A Fresh View of the World

Graeme Urwin

Graeme Urwin is a consultant urologist at York
Teaching Hospital NHS Foundation Trust.

John Sentamu writes:

*None of us is indestructible. When we are young we may kid
ourselves that we will live for ever, but in older age the reality
becomes more apparent!*

*In recent times, I have had the great privilege (if not pleasure!) to
see how wonderful the NHS is first-hand. I've had treatment for
salmonella, had my appendix removed and my shoulder operated
on. Our doctors and nurses do such a fantastic job caring for us and
keeping our spirits high in times of suffering – I am indebted to
them for their professionalism and devotion to duty.*

*We need to think holistically about health issues. In other words,
our well-being isn't just determined by how we are physically – we
also need to consider our mental and spiritual well-being. Our*

shared experience with those around us in our communities also helps to break down important barriers.

For me, it is crucial that we can identify with those around us, and show empathy. This is an important part of being able to share in the love of God. We are each made uniquely and have individual wisdom to offer, but we are also more than the sum of our parts – it is good that we live in co-dependency, with intertwined relationships. This is what binds us together.

We need to understand that in Christ we are all one body – and when a tiny toe hurts the entire body bends over to see what is wrong. We need to stop living as if we are individuals in isolation.

This chapter looks at the story of Graeme, a consultant urologist who has reflected on his own experiences of ill health so as to reach out to those who may not usually be prepared to discuss their own symptoms and difficulties through a series of men's health sessions within his community.

It's often said that spiritual transformation occurs in one of two ways, either through crisis or through prayer. Like most men, it took a crisis for me to rethink my life and my relationship with God. I don't want to sound melodramatic, but I almost died, and you don't come back from that sort of experience the way you went in.

Looking back, I can pinpoint when I had my first symptom. At the time I thought I'd eaten a dodgy curry. There were other symptoms too – hypertension, anxiety, headaches, blurred vision. I'd get tense and sometimes quite angry. Of course, everyone thought I was just Urwin, being grouchy as usual.

It was another two years, on Easter Monday 1998, before I was diagnosed with pheochromocytoma, a tumour of the adrenal gland. The tumour was found to be benign, but it was secreting an excess of adrenaline, the fight or flight hormone, into my body. That morning I woke up with the mother of all headaches and was vomiting every twenty minutes. My wife tried without any luck to get a doctor to come out to see me at our home, so we ended up driving to the drop-in centre. Thinking about it now, I probably should have gone straight to accident and emergency, but I was out of it, so we didn't think. When I got in the surgery, the doctor put the old blood pressure cuff on and clocked it at 280 over 230. Normally it would be 110 over 70, so I was desperately hypertensive. 'We had better get you into hospital,' he said.

'Good. I'm just off to be sick then.' I went off to the toilets and the next thing I know, I'm waking up on a hospital ward with a junior doctor doing a lumbar puncture.

Apparently, I blacked out and got wedged between the big white telephone and the door, so no one could get into the cubicle. That is part of the eight hours I can't account for at all. When I came round, I was put on some tablets to control my symptoms and stayed in hospital for about a week. Two weeks later I was back in again to have my adrenal gland excised, and thankfully I've been well since.

At the time I was so out of it that I didn't have a clue what was going on. It's only in retrospect that I look back and think, oh, I nearly died there. I'm a bit of a pragmatist, in so far as I'm of the theory, pick yourself up, dust yourself off and get on with it, but I know that coming out of that experience I was a different person to the one who went in.

As a surgeon I deal with people who are ill every day, but somehow it registered in a different way when it happened to me. It certainly affected my relationship with my patients. Having experienced serious illness myself, I feel more empathy towards those under my care. I understand what it's like because I've been there and I've done it. I've had a catheter, I've had drips, I've had lines in my neck and tubes down my throat – I know what it's about. I'm much more aware of the pressures patients are under and it has changed my practice. I realise the importance of simple things, like ensuring that patients get their results in a more timely fashion. It wasn't necessarily conscious, but I found that I was picking up the phone a lot more and talking to patients personally about their results, rather than having them wait four to six weeks for a clinic appointment, when they'd show up for a three o'clock slot, but because often I was running late they wouldn't get in until quarter-to-four. That wasn't the best for them. It was something little that I could change to help. It seems sensible to me now, basic human kindness, but I hadn't realised that before, I'd always been very much the traditionalist, of the view, come back and get your results after six weeks.

It was probably partly because of my crisis of health and partly because I'm getting older, and hopefully a little wiser too, that I started to view life differently. Thinking about my faith more deeply was part of that change. I suppose up until then you might say that I'd had quite a chequered faith journey. I was brought up in a very fundamentalist environment with the Brethren. Our church philosophy was, the Bible says it, God wrote it, it's therefore true, now get on with it. I was taught that salvation was a means to getting saved, however you define that, at some point in the future. I've moved away from that now. I suppose I started to question more what I believed and what my relationship with God meant to me, practically in my life. I started to read more around my faith and was particularly inspired by a Franciscan priest, Richard Rohr, who opened my eyes to the idea of exploring male spirituality. He also led me to consider more what I now believe is the authentic heart of the Gospel – the kingdom of God is at hand. I believe that if something is at hand, then it is here and now. Yes, the kingdom of God is in the future, but I believe we can live in the benefits of the kingdom now, and that means, health, wholeness and salvation, however you want to define it.

The idea of male spirituality led me to think more about men's health, because I felt that it wasn't just the spiritual side of life that men were neglecting. The general view is that men don't access the health service. They are fatalistic about their health and leave their symptoms until sadly for some it is too late. Sadly, the statistics support this view. Men die on average five years younger than women. A quarter of us will be dead before we're sixty-five. We take care of ourselves less, we're more prone to alcoholism, obesity, diabetes, cardiovascular disease and a host of other things.

I became passionate about healthy masculinity, of which physical health was one part, but it was only one part. We are all spiritual beings, but sometimes that needs teasing out. Then there was the idea of men as fathers and men as role models, which had always been important to me, mainly because of the inspiration I'd taken from various male figures in my own life.

I've been fortunate in having good role models who were able to inspire me and give me the bigger picture at various stages in my life. Even when I look back at my decision to go into medicine, you could call it chance, serendipity or divine intervention. We had a very progressive careers master at my grammar school and he would arrange work experience for us. I had a vague idea that I might like to do something about pharmacy or pharmacology. So he sent me off to a pharmaceutical company for a week. I lived in digs and it was nice being away from home and trying to look after myself for a week or so, but the job was pretty dull. Basically, it was just a load of rabbits sitting in cages with a thermometer rammed up their bottom and people were squirting drugs into them to see what effect it had. There was a guy there, he was old school, handlebar moustache, ex-RAF sort of thing. We were having a crack and he said: 'You don't want to be doing this sort of thing. If you do really want to get into it, you need to get into it via medicine, so do a medical degree first, and then if you like it, do that.'

It sounded like a good idea. It was just one of those meetings that turns you in the right direction, so that was it, I applied for medicine and I got in.

From the first few weeks I knew that I wanted to be a surgeon, but the specialism I chose was again down to a fortuitous meeting with a surgeon who inspired me. I got on with him and thought, hey, this is good, this is what I want to do. It's often how life works, we find someone who makes us see the world in a different way and that is where we turn.

I chatted through this idea with my vicar, about how we might work together to help men to look at their lives more holistically, and learn to take care of themselves so that they could enjoy life more fully. My vicar got in touch with Martin Wallace, the Bishop of Selby, and after talking it through with him, we decided to run an evening together where I would provide information on men's health and the Bishop would then talk about issues of male spirituality, and the role of fathers.

We booked a bar and put some flyers out. I wasn't sure what to expect, but out of courtesy I went to see some general practitioners in the local area to ask if they wanted to put a notice up about the event and also to give them a heads up that there may be an increase in the number of blokes coming forward for consultation on the back of the initiative. I didn't want them to feel blind-sided by some idiot in the community doing his own thing and increasing their workload.

At our first event, about sixty men turned up, ranging in age from sixteen to eighty. There were certainly loads of blokes who wouldn't normally walk into a church. Probably because we had beer, but you then have to rewind and look at the sorts of situations where you found Jesus. Almost always it was with food and he reserved his criticism for the Pharisees on the Sabbath, but all the rest, almost always you'd find him with the marginalised, eating and drinking – there's something in that.

I talked about lifestyle issues, sexual health, adolescent health and specifics like prostate problems, cardiovascular disease, alcohol, smoking and weight. The Bishop then took on the issues of male spirituality, and fathers as role models. We've done subsequent gigs, we did one entitled, 'Beer, Nuts and Bishops', which was a rather tongue-in-cheek way of describing the evening, but was a similar type of format.

On the basis of the first meeting a guy went to have a prostate check-up and he was found to have prostate cancer and has had successful treatment as a result, so it did make a difference. So often in life we don't know what difference we are making, so when I see someone benefit from what I've been able to do, I feel very thankful. I have a great job. I'm semi-retired now, but I still get a sense of reward from doing my work, even after all these years. If I can put people at their ease then so much the better, because I'm dealing with some very frightened people and often doing extraordinarily intimate things to them. I just stand back in wonder sometimes and think, you're actually going to let me do that to you? You don't know me, and yet you trust me. It's an enormous place of privilege. As part of my job I do a bit of teaching to fifth-year medical students. I always try to inculcate in them the notion that it's a privilege to do this job. If they don't feel that, then they are in the wrong game and they should do something else – it's as important as that.

15 When the Impossible becomes Possible

Beryl Beynon

Beryl Beynon OBE is Medical Director of the Jacob's Well Appeal in Beverley, a registered charity which supplies medical relief overseas. Beryl set up the charity with her husband Peter in 1984, to send aid to hospitals in Poland. Since then, the charity's work has expanded across Eastern Europe, Asia, Lebanon and Africa.

John Sentamu writes:

As followers of an all-powerful living God, we should expect the unexpected – nothing is routine.

We are rarely told in advance what God might do but we are promised that God has the power to change any situation. The first step is to fear no evil. Not to be afraid. He is in control.

Jesus encouraged people to feed the hungry and clothe the naked, not to walk by on the other side when they saw someone in trouble. Practical steps to tackle need and suffering.

When I was growing up, we never had much money but we were gloriously happy. In tough times my father gave away what he had to support others. Because of his generosity, and the kindness of others like him, no one in the village went hungry and no one died. We recognised that as a community we would sink or swim together – or to use modern parlance, we were 'all in this together'.

As Christians, let us focus on the task in hand rather than looking too far down the line for what we think might happen. The future will look after itself. As the saying goes: The best laid schemes of mice and men …

This chapter looks at the story of Beryl who, with her husband Peter, has helped to bring aid and hope to people living in Poland, Afghanistan and Romania. We follow their journey gathering medicines and hear about the life-changing differences their contribution makes.

✢

When I first started sending medical aid to Poland during a harsh period of martial law, I had no idea where it would lead me. If I'd known thirty years ago what I know now, like the prophet Jonah, I probably would have run away.

Thankfully, God doesn't let us see the whole picture at once. If he did, we'd most likely think our task impossible. Over the years help and supplies appeared when they were needed, in a way that was really miraculous. Yet, while some people might call it fortunate coincidence, I believe that the way things happen isn't just by chance. When I look back on the work of the Jacob's Well Appeal, I can see the hand of God in the networking of everything, and it has been a tremendous privilege to be a part of it.

My initial interest in Poland was sparked from many directions. I grew up in Hyde, a small mill town in Greater Manchester. After the war my grandmother housed three Polish men who had fled to escape the Communist regime and were working in the cotton mill. She lived in a small two-up, two-down terrace, and the men shared a bedroom which had no furniture except the three beds they slept in. A sister of one of the men would write to us, asking if we could send various things she needed, so I knew that it was difficult to get the most basic of conveniences in Poland at that time. Later the sister got cancer and had a colostomy. She wrote to say that she had no bags to collect the waste and asked if we could find some and send them to her. I realised then, she had no other option; we were it.

My family wasn't very well off, but my two sisters and I were always well loved and cared for. We lived on rations during the war and for some time afterwards, but while we didn't have much, we had enough. I passed my 11-plus to go to the local grammar school. I wanted to be a nurse, because coming from a lower social class it never entered my head that I could be a doctor. It was the school that encouraged me to try, so I worked very hard and won a state scholarship to Manchester University Medical School.

It was during my first year at university that I started to look for God. I had no real faith up to this point, apart from a few years in a Congregationalist Sunday school, so I decided to sample several churches and eventually got confirmed. Shortly after that Peter asked me out and he was a big distraction, in a good way. He was training to be a lay reader and was studying medicine in the same year as me, so we had a lot in common. We got engaged as soon as we passed our finals, and almost a year later we were married.

It wasn't until many years later, when our children were teenagers, that I began to think about the hardship in Poland again. The need of the people was brought to my attention by an appeal from Christian Aid for money to buy medicines and equipment for Polish hospitals. At the time, it didn't seem right for us to just give money. If we'd have given £1,000 it would have bought virtually nothing in terms of medical supplies, I knew that. However, I wanted to do something to help, and that feeling wouldn't go away.

Within a week of me deciding to do something all of the links miraculously fell into place. We knew a Polish GP and his wife who had escaped after the war and ended up, not happily we think, in England. They were desperate to help and put me in touch with a couple in Redcar who had already sent a truck full of medical aid to Lodz's paediatric hospital, in central Poland. We joined forces and very soon I was gathering supplies.

The hospital in Poland asked for drip sets and intravenous cannulae. I went to our hospital stores to ask where I could buy some. As it turned out, they were throwing some away, which we could have for free. I left with seventy drip sets. It was my first lesson in faith, and there were many more on the way.

As technology was updated or prescriptions changed it meant that there were lots of medicines and equipment that couldn't be used any more by the NHS. I realised that no one was thinking to rescue these, and it was such a waste in one sense. Donated medicines can be passed on after careful checking and documenting, provided there is adequate shelf life left to meet the recipient's regulations and requirements and the condition is good. As for technology, it might be old equipment to us, but a lot of the time it is much better than the equipment being used in some other countries. It is also often cheaper to operate than the latest equipment and therefore better suited to their conditions.

Soon hospitals started to ask us for what they needed. In Gdansk, on the Baltic coast, a hospital asked us for catheters, which could be used to dialyse children with renal failure because you can't do it through veins when they're small, it's just not possible. These were £50 each and the hospital wanted two different sizes. I tried to order just a few to start with, but I could only order them in tens. So, I ordered £1,000 worth, which amounted to two shoe box sizes. It was what they'd asked for but I wasn't happy about the purchase. In terms of cost it seemed very expensive, for what looked like very little.

The charity couldn't be spending that kind of money on such a small amount of equipment again. Some time later we made a trip to that same hospital and as we arrived a baby was placed into my arms. 'This is Machek,' a nurse told me, 'he's five months old. He wouldn't be here without your catheters.' Suddenly, the catheters didn't seem so expensive after all.

Visiting Poland and seeing the conditions the medical staff were working in did us a tremendous amount of good. It can be easy to get into the habit of complaining, but we returned home with an immense feeling that we had nothing to grumble about. At the time the Polish people were living under militia law and everything was rationed. Growing up during the war I was used to rationing, but this seemed to be worse than our real wartime conditions, because families in Poland often didn't receive the rations allocated to them.

Landing back on British soil, I felt an enormous sense of freedom. Even the most run-down areas at home looked beautiful in comparison, mainly because the shops had goods in them – simple things we take for granted like being able to walk by a butchers and see meat in the window.

During the next two years we learned a lot – how to gather medicines, how to store them, how to move them, the logistics of shipping a container and how to get the money to do it – and in 1984, the Jacob's Well Polish Appeal was registered with the Charity Commissioners. In the same period, I'd expanded my GP surgery and opened a Christian bookshop in the space that was left at the front. This proved very useful as a centre to bring everything together for the charity, and as things progressed we opened a charity shop upstairs.

We kept on working in Poland until after the revolution in 1989, when the Polish government started to say that the value of our aid had to be deducted from the hospital budget. We didn't expect the hospital directors to take £100,000 off their budget. It would mean that they would have no money left to pay their staff. It was disappointing all round, but at least now they were free, which was the one thing the people always said they wanted.

By that time another door had opened in Romania via a visiting priest to our parish who told us about families needing milk and supplies. Romania was very much poorer than Poland, and controls over freedom of speech were even tighter. When we visited, our hotel room was bugged and everywhere we went we were watched and followed. A policeman was posted to the entrance to our hotel and there were more police on every road junction, who would radio ahead to tell their colleagues we were on our way.

Many of the Romanian doctors were too scared to speak to us to let us know what was needed. Eventually when we started to get a bit more successful at getting supplies in, whatever we sent would be interfered with before it arrived at the hospital. For example, we sent a scanner that had a probe, and when it arrived the probe was missing, which meant that the equipment couldn't be used. It became embarrassing because everything we sent out was damaged in some way by the time it arrived.

It became increasingly frustrating and dangerous. Romanian spies bugged the phones in our home and in my GP surgery. We had one or two strange people call, who were obviously from abroad trying to find out about us. Then one day when I was in the dentist, a Dacia, a Romanian car, pulled up outside. I couldn't believe this was happening, not in Beverley, our quiet little East Riding Town. I thought they had definitely come to get me this time. Thankfully I was ok, but after about eighteen months of working in Romania my husband and I started to get warnings that if we carried on something would happen to us – that we would be killed if we carried on. Ultimately we decided, after consulting with the British Embassy, that it was time to stop. Not long afterwards the Romanian Communist dictator, Ceaucescu, was assassinated.

Again, just as we stopped aid to one country, another door opened and we started going into Afghanistan, where life got even more dangerous. In the early days in Afghanistan there were bombs going off and rockets blowing about. In the civil war, many houses were destroyed. We did feel afraid, but we just had to have some faith in the Lord and trust that he wouldn't let us down. Whatever had happened in the past, he had always been there for us.

Both Peter and I are seventy-six years old now. I still run a small private practice and keep revalidating my medical licence so that we can do this work. However, we are obviously not going to be able to do this for ever, and we would like others to be able to take it on, if possible. Whether or not that will happen, I don't know. We've been fortunate that the Lord has led us the way that he's wanted us to go. Now we hope that the next generation will listen to the messages that come and not be afraid to follow them.

Lee Kirkby

Lee Kirkby is Youth Minister at Beverley Minster. He runs the Youth Cafe Project, which attracts more than 250 young people every month.

John Sentamu writes:

People often say that young people are our leaders of tomorrow, but they aren't, they are the leaders of today!

So often our young people are the ones who are not only offering solutions to the problems being faced by our society, but also offering their time and effort to help deliver a positive outcome.

Our press is consistently stigmatising the contribution of young people to society, but I have seen time and again their willingness to serve and transform communities for the better.

We should never forget the importance of education – not just for the individual, but also for society. We should all want to see a better educated society, where all matter, and all can fulfil their potential.

But education, whether that be academic or vocationally based, is not about cramming information in, it is about nurturing the individual and ensuring that they flourish. It is about bringing the best out of people.

Rather than asking how much we spend on educating our young people, we should ask ourselves what the cost is of not educating them properly. We need to invest in each other and trust that with support and encouragement transformation is possible.

Communities thrive when we build relationships and truly value each other. However, when we view each other with suspicion and doubt, that is when communities struggle and become dysfunctional.

This chapter looks at the story of Lee, a youth minister who has found new ways to build relationships between the church and young people in the town of Beverley.

❖

A lot of people are surprised to find out that I am a Christian, especially a Christian youth minister. 'You?' they'll say, incredulously, as if it couldn't possibly be true. I guess they have an idea of what a Christian minister should look like or how they should behave, and that image isn't me. I don't wear sandals with socks or have long Jesus hair. I don't pretend to be someone high and mighty. I'm a human being the same as everyone else. Sometimes that means allowing myself to make mistakes and not being afraid to own up to them. I love people and relating to people about everyday things, which means having a joke and not taking myself too seriously. I'd like to say that I'm daring. Not in a way that I'm naughty with my faith, but I'm not afraid to portray the God that I believe in, in an informal way that isn't all about long words from the Bible or stern images of the big man upstairs. My God is a personal God and the best way for me to express that is in how I live my life and behave towards other people, even if it that isn't always the way that other people might expect.

However we choose to live there will always be expectations of us. When I was in Sixth Form there was a lot of pressure on me to go to university, because all my friends were and it was what everyone did at that age. I'm not the most academic person. I'm quite capable of doing academic work, but I'm far happier rolling my sleeves up and getting stuck in on a job. At the time I went through the motions of applying to university and chose a course in theology and religious studies, because that's what I was interested in. I applied because that was what I thought I was supposed to do, but at the same time I didn't feel in my heart that I wanted to go away and study. In the end I didn't take up the university offer and instead decided to take a gap year, working as a teaching assistant and getting involved in youth ministry at Beverley Minster.

I really enjoyed what I was doing and realised that I wanted to pursue youth ministry. My own youth workers had been a real inspiration to me and I felt that I would like to give the same to the next generation, to invest in other people's lives. There was still a nagging in the back of my head to get a degree or some formal qualification. It was a pressure I couldn't really ignore and it made me feel torn. Then I came across the Centre for Youth Ministry, which allowed me to combine my hands-on youth work with an academic course. It was the ideal solution for me, because it meant that I could study and also keep my job in youth ministry.

If I hadn't followed my heart to take a gap year then it is very unlikely that I would be doing what I'm doing now. I listen to my heart a lot and it speaks volumes. It is my way of discerning what God wants for my life. When I was first learning about God at youth ministry, I'd often feel him speak to me through my heart. When I was a chorister I sat through so many services and listened to sermons that seemed to go on and on without making any sense. In contrast, the youth leaders communicated to me in a way that made a 2000-year-old text relevant to my life. Their energy and passion for the Gospel inspired me. Whatever topic they were talking about that week, I felt that message had some meaning for my life. In my mind it was God speaking to my heart through the youth leader. I'd go away thinking, 'Yeah, God is real, he is a personal God and he wants to speak to me.'

I found the youth leaders an inspiration in other ways too. For a start, they didn't look like I expected a church minister to look. They were cool and popular. They were enjoying life and weren't embarrassed or ashamed about being a Christian, so why should I be? Of course, at age sixteen there were a lot of conflicting pressures. How did I separate being a Christian from living for the world? There was a lot of peer pressure to go out to parties and get involved in behaviour that probably wasn't what God would've liked me to be doing. After a few months of being involved in that kind of activity I felt something inside my head telling me that it wasn't quite right. Turning up to church on a Sunday morning with a hangover probably isn't the best way to be. I didn't want to keep doing that, but to stop meant making tough decisions about how I lived my life. It's not easy, but sometimes you've got to make those choices, even if it means being unpopular with your friends. At times in my late teens I was envious of friends who seemed to be having a great time doing all kinds of things, but on reflection, I can honestly say that I loved my life as a young person and have never regretted for one day living life the way I did.

Growing up I was one of maybe ten young people in a church congregation of about two hundred and fifty. By the time I became a youth minister there were just two of us. Where were all the young people? Perhaps it had something to do with the time of the service. What young person would want to get up early on a Sunday morning to sit with a group of strangers in a church service that maybe didn't relate to their life in any way? As an alternative we set up a mid week evening service for young people that was more relaxed and used media and technology to get them involved. Now, about thirty young people attend the mid week service and it has been really encouraging to see some adults coming along too, who, without being aware of it, are sharing their wisdom and becoming role models for some of the younger ones.

The Youth Cafe project grew out of our church youth group in 2006. At the time we had about twenty teenagers coming along to the youth group, which was purely church and faith based. The group expressed an interest in having somewhere they could bring their non-Christian friends, which wouldn't be intimidating or leave them thinking, what's all this God stuff about? So, we came up with an idea of a purely social youth cafe event where we'd serve hot chocolate and home-made cakes. It was basically a drop-in where teenagers could chill out, listen to music, eat a bit of food and talk. About fifteen people turned up at the first event. Six weeks later we ran another one and this time the numbers doubled to thirty. At the third event there were one hundred young people, and by our eighth Youth Cafe night we had three hundred people through the doors with more outside desperate to get in.

That night took us completely by surprise. When we started out we never expected the Youth Cafe idea to be so popular. There wasn't any event for young people like it in Beverley at the time – obviously we scratched an itch and the young people responded. It wasn't that the Minster wasn't big enough to accommodate that many people, but we didn't have the supervision we needed. We tried to explain this when we shut the doors, saying, 'Sorry we can't let any more in, it's just not safe.' The result was a huge commotion on the steps of Beverley Minster with young people banging on the door shouting, 'Why can't we come into the church? We should be allowed in church.'

When the rest of the church got wind of what had happened they were naturally worried and called a meeting. I was sure that would be the end of the Youth Cafe, but to my surprise the church decided to embrace the fact that so many young people wanted to be involved in the event. They wanted to affirm all the good work the Youth Cafe had achieved, but obviously couldn't risk having the same problems happen again. Things would have to change. An event of this size needed policies and structures in place. We needed more stewards to supervise, we needed to know what we would do if there were behavioural issues or if someone turned up drunk. There were also the parents to deal with at the end of the night, which could mean two or three hundred people turning up in cars. Practical things like that I hadn't thought about when we set off, but now we have the police involved to initiate a one-way system around the Minster to deal with the traffic.

These days the Youth Cafe is not so much a cafe as a huge youth event, which attracts an average of 250 people every month. We have staging where the young people showcase their bands, sing and dance. We also have a DJ, giant inflatables, sumo wrestling and gladiator jousting, as well as the home-made buns and hot chocolates that started us off. Another big change is that we have to charge. As the event expanded it was the only way to carry on, because the funds we had available to us wouldn't support an event of that size. At the time, I worried that charging would affect numbers, but it hasn't. In a way it has professionalised the event. People want to come. They get a printed ticket and it is something to go to. It is something to look forward to and because we generate our own income, we don't need to worry about where the funds are coming from each month, and can put this money back into making the event even better.

On the weeks when there is no Youth Cafe we've also set up a smaller free event on a Friday night which we call, Night Cafe. In a way, it is what the Youth Cafe was when it started. There is a bit of background music and we serve coffee, hot chocolate and home-made cakes. It's a small intimate space where proper conversations can happen. We don't get everyone who comes to the monthly event, but we get about thirty young people along, and that is thirty young people we are getting to know and building relationships with.

A lot of people say to me, but there's no faith aspect, why are you doing it? In a way I don't think that matters. I see what we are doing as helping to break down stereotypes of who Christians are, what church can be and what it means to have faith. For some people, even walking into a church can be intimidating. Through Youth Cafe, young people who might have never been in a church before are able to walk into this massive building, hear the music and feel at home straight away. It also helps us as youth ministers when we go into schools, because lots of the pupils recognise us from the Youth Cafe and relate to us immediately through that.

The Youth Cafe is reaching out to the wider community and in doing so the church is too. When a 14-year-old girl committed suicide in Beverley we knew that there would be hundreds of young people who we knew and worked with through Youth Cafe feeling lost and upset. Using social media the youth team at the Minster put a message out to let people know that Beverley Minster would be open between nine o'clock and midnight if anyone wanted to come and light a candle or just spend some private time in prayer. Even if one person found space to just be and spend time with God to help them come to terms with what had happened, it would have been worth it. By the end of the night we had just short of two hundred people through the doors – all young people who had come to the Youth Cafe, and because it was late at night they brought their parents.

That night we opened the church and the young people felt completely safe and at home coming in. They were coming back into the place where on Friday they were dancing, and now it was somewhere to reflect, to mourn and ask God the difficult questions. When I see people coming together like that I realise that this is what church is about. It is about community and supporting each other. Without the Youth Cafe, we might not have been able to do that.

17 Living Out Your Faith

Alison Phillipson

The Revd Alison Phillipson is Vicar of Coatham and Dormanstown parish in Redcar. Six months after joining the parish Alison set up The Church Shop, which serves both as a source of income for the parish and a mission outreach into the community.

John Sentamu writes:

Living our faith isn't about what we wear or about what we say, it is about how we practically live our lives, the decisions we take and what we actually end up doing.

They say actions speak louder than words, and if we want to show God's love in action then we need to get out in our local communities and serve others in practical ways.

*Did you know that more people volunteer for church organisa-
tions and activities than any other group or organisation in the
country? The church has been doing the Big Society for over 2000
years!*

*In this chapter we hear the story of how a local church in
Dormanstown set up a shop in its local community. This is a place
not just where people can buy second-hand goods at a fair price –
but also somewhere where people can come and seek support over
a cup of tea. We need to reach out in new ways, showing God's love
to all.*

*It's important that as a church we don't wait for people to come
to us, but we go out and meet them where they are.*

✣

How can we be a disciple today? It's a question that all Christians ask, but sometimes I think we can look too hard for the
answer. You might say that it's easy for me in a sense. I'm a
Reverend. People see the dog collar, they know who I am and
they know what to expect from me. There is an expectation
that I will talk about God. People feel able to ask me questions
about faith and expect that if they do, then I'll answer them.
When you're a regular lay member of the congregation then the
role isn't always so clear. People don't expect you to talk about
God and if you do, they can find that uncomfortable.

Often people find it difficult to talk about their faith, because
they worry that if they do others might think they're mad.
Sometimes we can worry too much about knowing the right
thing to say or making the grand gestures. I don't want to see
my congregation standing on soap boxes, preaching about
Jesus. It is our actions that are important. People will ask me,
but what can I do? Well, we can't all go off to save the world in
Africa. As much as we admire the people who do, we don't all
have those opportunities. Yet, that doesn't mean that we can't
make a difference where we are. There is so much we can do
every day. I see so many people in my parish who are living out

their faith in very quiet ways. They ask how can I be a disciple, but they already are, they are doing it without even realising. Simply being kind to a neighbour or helping someone with their shopping, if your motivation is your faith, then in doing that you're being a disciple.

In my parish most people don't come to church on a Sunday. They will come in huge numbers to support each other at baptisms and funerals, but aside from that they are not interested in crossing the threshold. As a regular churchgoer it can be hard to understand how daunting walking into a church can be for some people. I used to work in the police force so I am used to dealing with people at all levels and in all kinds of situations. I suppose you could say that doing that job has helped to keep my feet on the floor, yet, I still know that when people see my dog collar it can make them uneasy. I visited a family to organise a man's funeral recently, and when I was leaving the deceased's daughter said to me, 'We were so nervous when you were coming, we didn't know what to expect, but it's been great. It's been so easy to talk to you and you're so nice. It wasn't what we were expecting.'

Sadly, so many people assume that they are going to be condemned by the church, so it can be a breath of fresh air when they find out they are not. When you come alongside people and try to understand where they are, then you're not going to condemn. One of my favourite phrases from my mother is, there is more than one way to skin a cat. If you treat people with respect, regardless of their lifestyle then you can gently help them to change, if that's what they want to do.

God never fails to surprise me with the many ways in which he reaches into people's lives. When I first became Vicar of Coatham and Dormanstown in 2009, the parish was heading towards bankruptcy. We had two churches to run and a dwindling congregation. The situation was desperate and I knew that I would have to make some money if we were to survive. I'd heard that, in the distant past, the parish had once run a charity shop. I didn't know anything about running a shop of any kind, but I decided it might be something worth trying again. Of course, I didn't do all the work, I just gave the support and said let's get on with it.

We found premises in the Farndale Square area of Dorman-stown and arranged with the council to let us rent it as a charity shop, which we called simply, The Church Shop. The Archbish-op's Mission Fund gave us a grant to help set up and members of the congregation helped out with the decorating. Everyone was very enthusiastic, but in my mind I was thinking, how are we going to make this work, where on earth will we get the stock? I needn't have worried. Soon afterwards people who had never even been to church came and asked if they could help out, either by volunteering in the shop or donating goods. People were so generous, and before long we had more stock than we knew what to do with.

I was amazed at how it all came together, and how quickly people who have no interest in church accepted, trusted and valued us as The Church Shop. It was important to me that we were seen as a part of the church and were not just about making money. We needed to cover our overheads, of course, if we were to stay open, but as far as I was concerned, people gave us the stuff to sell, so any profit was a bonus. It meant that we could keep our prices low and also that we could use space, which other shops might need for stock, as a community area, for people to sit together, have a cup of tea and a chat.

I've found that people who wouldn't come to church to look for someone to talk to will come into the shop because it feels safe to them. People come in and browse, they get the feel of the place and then if they feel welcome they might have a cuppa and talk. Often I'll go in and the shop is packed with people sitting chatting – it is really lovely to see.

There are a lot of lonely people who don't have someone just to natter to about everyday things. In a world where people won't stop and listen, we are here and we will listen. Some people come in a couple of times a day, just to take time out, read the paper and chat to whoever is there. If anyone specifi-cally wants to speak to me as a vicar, then I get their details and

I will go to their house to see them. Mostly people just want someone to talk to, to enjoy everyday chatter, because they live on their own. It's been good in that way for some of our volunteers too. Some of the people who volunteer live on their own or have lost confidence in work, and they blossom in the shop, it has given them a new lease of life.

Of course, it's never been the case that God was only to be found in the church, but often that's people's perception. Having the shop has enabled us to take God out into the community in a visible way and given people an opportunity to live out their faith in a practical sense. It's great to see people growing in faith and in confidence. The shop has surpassed all my expectations in that respect. It's shown me how all the small things we do fit together to fulfil Jesus' commandment to love one another. Simple things, like serving somebody a cup of coffee in the shop and sitting down and listening to them, are important. Rather than seeing these as small things, we need to thank people and let them know that they're doing a good job, because what they are doing is not small in its impact, it is affecting ordinary people's lives. When we meet people for the first time in the shop, we don't know who they are. They might be a bit cantankerous, but we don't know what they've been through. For us, as The Church Shop, it's about gently talking to people and listening to them. We've got really good staff who understand that we're here to serve in a much wider sense than just over a counter and most people value that.

Often we never know how we've influenced somebody else's life. We will do something or say something, then we move on and the other person moves on. That's how life is. Yet, we can all influence somebody else's life for good or for ill, just by what we say. We can all think of someone in our life who has had a great influence on us. In many cases that person won't even realise the impact they've had. To them, it could be a seemingly insignificant encounter, yet we remember it and it affects how we live our lives. For that reason, the big question I always ask is, how did I treat somebody? Is it how Jesus would have treated them, and if not, why not? What would Jesus do?

How would Jesus react? The answer is always, with love. He might say that a person should be changing their ways, but that message was always given with love, he never condemned anyone.

What we want is for people on the outside of church to look at people on the inside and think, wow, what have they got? I know they haven't got a right happy life in some respects, they've got health problems and worries just like me. So, what makes them glow the way they do? Whatever it is, I want some of it. That is what discipleship is about, and that is what The Church Shop has helped us to achieve. We are planting seeds, we're showing people that God cares, he's in the community and loves everyone equally, whether they go to church or not. As for the future, who knows where those seeds will grow. I don't, but I know that they will.

18 God-Given Talents

Robin Gamble

Robin Gamble is Vicar of Holy Trinity Church, Idle in Bradford and the diocesan evangelist. Robin uses popular culture to make God accessible to those outside the church, by running events such as 'The Gospel according to Queen', 'Bart Simpson meets Jesus' and 'The Beatles Bible'.

John Sentamu writes:

God wants to use our individual talents, skills and interests in transforming the lives of individuals, communities and ourselves in new ways. No one is too young or too old to play their part.

Serving God is rarely dull. I have found the more I trust God, the more of an adventure life can be!

We need to recognise the gifts God has given us to reach out to others – not constantly focus on the things we can't do. For example, I doubt I will ever play football for Manchester United now, but does that mean my life is a failure and that I should be downhearted? No!

Doubt is natural. It is OK to question God – even to be angry at him – he can handle it! But we should not forget that God made everyone a wonderfully and fearfully created unique individual. Stop trying to be someone else and celebrate the person you are. We are all one body, but all different parts.

At the Olympics, Mo Farah proved he was the best 5,000- and 10,000-metre runner in the world but I suspect if he raced Usain Bolt over 100 or 200 metres he would lose by a long way. We need to recognise our strengths and concentrate on being the best we can be.

This chapter looks at the story of Robin, an 'unchurchy' vicar who uses popular culture and his own life experiences to reach out to others.

✢

I've never been able to get that churchy, which is a difficulty for a vicar. I always found the family of the church, the people, fantastic, but when it came to church services, I don't know why, I just found them so dull and heavy, almost painful. Church was like the TARDIS to me – time stood still. I'd look at my watch and couldn't believe that I'd only been in an hour, in real time I was sure it should be mid-afternoon.

When I was growing up it would take me three days to recover from a church service. Twice in one day, every day, was a potential nightmare scenario for me, but that was what I found myself doing at theological college. Of course, I had to play the game at college and pretend I was really enjoying going along to a service at 7.20 a.m. and again at 6 p.m. I had to pretend that it was deeply meaningful and that through the service God was speaking to me, but it wasn't and he wasn't.

When I looked around, everyone else at theological college was sensational. They were always reading the Bible and saying their prayers. In comparison, I was flipping useless at it. I felt so unbelievably unspiritual. I was so not ready or young or worldly or whatever. Thankfully, for me, my calling was never about being this great pure spiritual man. Rather, it was about telling other people about God. Since I'd become a Christian, I'd spent eighteen months telling everyone about Jesus and trying to make my life a bit better. I thought it was normal to say, 'Wow, God's absolutely fantastic'. I didn't realise that most other Christians didn't do this.

I had experienced God working in my own life. I knew God was amazing, that he was the great life-changer. His forgiveness had turned me around, from being an unruly teen who was expelled from school, to being more of the person I wanted to be. During my five years at theological college, I never lost sight of that. Surely it was possible to make church and worshipping and joining with other Christians reflect that incredible experience? I didn't know how to do it, but I wanted to do it. It somehow didn't feel right that we had all this stuff that we had to get through, so to speak. I resolved that when I got out I'd try to make going to church a fantastic, or, at least, a good experience. I wanted church to reflect what God is like. For me God was about people, not about church. I thought it's not enough to just go on doing religious experiences for people who come to the church, we've got to break out of that, get into where people are and find ways of communicating the Christian message and experience. In Mark's gospel it says, 'the common people heard him gladly'. More than anything else, that is what I wanted to achieve. I don't get there a lot of the time, but after more than thirty years in ministry, it's what I'm still aiming for.

If you put God at the centre, then the Gospel pops up all over the place. I'll be listening to music, reading a book or watching a film and suddenly I'll hear the voice of God in it, usually in the form of a question, asking, what is life all about?

The idea for 'The Gospel According to Queen', came while I was watching the film *Highlander*, when I heard the Queen song, 'Who Wants to Live Forever'. I was never a great fan of Queen, and I hadn't heard that song before, but there it was, playing as a soundtrack to the film and I just thought wow, if that isn't a gospel song, I don't know what is. Who wants to live forever? It's the ultimate question, and you can turn it around to 'Who wants to go to heaven?'

I used the idea at an Easter service. I showed lots of photographs I'd taken of people, while playing the music, and then I talked about who wants to live forever. People loved it. So I started to listening to other Queen songs and I found some of the lyrics provided an opportunity to make deep spiritual statements about the human condition without using traditional religious language. Songs such as 'I Want It All', 'I Want to Break Free', and 'You're My Best Friend'. From there it grew into a multi-media service with dance, live music and film, and we ended up taking it to theatres and reaching hundreds of people who are normally a million miles away from God, it was amazing.

As a vicar I'm always thinking, how do I make this interesting, how do I make this service alive to people? It's a wrestle every week and I'm still working on it. This morning I wrote a little piece about the television programme *Downton Abbey*, because at the end of the day, seven million people are watching every Sunday. Quite frankly there are more people in my parish watching *Downton Abbey* than reading the Bible on a Sunday night. If I want to connect, then I need to meet people where they are. It's rather like Jesus with his parables. Jesus says, look at that farmer, now what can we learn from him?

I'm always learning, always thinking what would Jesus do? When I was younger I was convinced that the Gospel was the only way for people. Now I've discovered that there are no clear answers. Life is always a yes and no. I had years of doubt, and this was weird for an evangelist, calling people to Jesus and inwardly thinking, I hope you're going to be there for them. I can't say what triggered these thoughts. My daughter was born with severe learning difficulties, but while this might have aggravated how I was feeling, I don't think it triggered it. Maybe it was just that everyone goes through a moment of intellectually starting to question, and maybe up to that point, I'd never been through that. I'm not sure, but once I had these feelings I couldn't shift them. They were like an inner voice, bouncing off the inside of my brain, and I didn't feel that I could tell anyone about this doubt I had, because what would that say about me and everything I'd done in my life?

When I first had these doubts they shook everything I believed. At times I felt I was hanging on to faith by the skin of my teeth. It took me a long time to realise that my doubt was actually more about me and my psychological make-up than about God. I'm prone to depression and massive personal insecurities, always expecting everything I do to fail, which is a doubt too in a sense.

Doubt isn't about saying, oh, I'm a really clever person, I've worked it all out about God and found he's a bit lacking. You can have blind doubt, just like you can have blind faith. We have this idea that people who have faith don't think rationally and people who have doubt do think rationally. But doubt is as irrational as faith. Loads of times I had doubt, but it wasn't based on rational intellectual analysis, it was based on an emotional fear.

It took me a long time to work all this out, because I didn't feel there was anybody that I could really share my thoughts with. I tried to solve my doubt by being introverted, all the time trying to think it through for myself. I read every book I could find that dealt with the existence of God. None of them helped. No matter how much I read I am never going to find an equation for the existence or non-existence of God. I now read the New Atheists and I can almost see in a flash how thin and emotional the arguments are, because I've been there so often. I've realised the only way to get out of this spiral is to stop focusing on myself and to start ministering to other people. Trying to sort God out, in an introverted way, didn't reveal anything to me. God only became real to me, when I stopped trying to sort him out and instead got involved with other people. I can't offer an adequate explanation why, it's just how it was for me.

Doubt was something I had to work through and think, it's ok, God's a big boy and just because I have my doubts, it's not going to knock him over. He can look after himself can God, no matter how much I doubt him. In the end I've just accepted that faith and doubt are bedfellows, almost. If you've not got any doubt then you've got certainty. If your faith is based on intellectual certainty, you're wobbly. The disciples had doubt. They were always doubting Jesus, asking questions. Jesus says how much greater faith those who never see me yet still believe. Well, I'm one of them.

Even if there isn't a God, it's unbelievable how the idea of God can transform your life. Some people will say it's just a psychological trick, but if it's just a psychological trick, could it be this real? If the idea of God so changes my life, how can it be that an idea, which is only a concept, changes my life so much for the better? I remember thinking quite soon after becoming a Christian that it's almost like the difference between seeing a black and white world and a colour world. It's like Plato's Cave, if you live in a world of shadows in a black and white world and that's all you've ever seen, that's ok. But if somebody shows you a colour photograph you suddenly think, woah, I'd like to be there.

The Bible says we're made in the image of God, we've been designed to have God at our core, so it's no surprise that human life works better when we put God at our centre because we've been designed to live that way. Just about every single aspect of the human condition becomes richer and deeper when you have a healthy relationship with God – your physical health, your relationships, your friendships, your attitude towards your work, your attitude towards the environment, your longevity, and your inner confidence. God is about joy. Believing is a happier way, a more joyful way, it's a healthier way. Life works out so much better. It has in my experience, anyway, and that's all I can do, share my own experience and talk to people about what they want in life. If they've got it all then they don't need God, but I don't think there are many out there who have got it all.

19 Life's Choices

Edwin Pugh

Professor Edwin Pugh MBE is a consultant in palliative medicine. For more than twenty years he has been involved in overseas missions with his wife, Kim, leading medical teams in Cambodia, Rwanda, Iran and Ukraine.

John Sentamu writes:

I often find when people say things to God like 'Don't send me there, anywhere but there!', that will be where they eventually find themselves volunteering to go. God has a fantastic sense of humour, and he knows what is best for our lives.

Life is like a long journey where there are many paths to take. Some paths are more winding than others, and you can't necessarily see the destination, but we can have confidence that while we travel with God our footing will be sure and secure.

When you follow God, everything can be a great adventure, but we need to learn to trust him.

Don't think of God like some big fruit machine in the sky, where we put our prayers in one end and expect our desired result to come out of the other. It simply doesn't work like that. You can't second guess what he is doing.

This chapter looks at the story of Edwin, a man who despite not wanting to travel has spent more than twenty years working overseas with his wife serving others. He explains how volunteering with refugees has taught him what 'vocation' really means.

I don't believe that there is always a right and a wrong when it comes to life's choices. There isn't only one door to go through. Opportunities come along and you have to decide whether to take them or not. Sometimes it might work out, sometimes it might not, but it may lead you to something else. What that might be, we can't tell. All I know is that God has a sense of humour with me, because I've always had my own thoughts about what I'd like to do, and then something else comes along that's different, but right for me.

If I'd had my way, I'd never have become a doctor. I wanted to work in computing, but at the time my mother thought there was no future in it. We laugh about that now. Instead she persuaded me to apply for medical school. Being a doctor wasn't what I saw myself doing when I was in the lower sixth form, but I applied to Newcastle Medical School and I got in. When I got there it was hard work, mainly because I'd taken maths at A level instead of biology at A level, so felt that I was behind before I'd even started. I did not enjoy my medical training in the first few years, but looking back, I made it; it's been my life and I wouldn't swap it.

It was while at medical school that I met my wife, Kim. She was a strong Christian and taught me what it meant to be in relationship with God. I'd grown up in an Anglican home and you could say that I had a good Christian upbringing. I knew there was something there and I went to church on Sunday, but I didn't connect that with my life in terms of a relationship with God. Then I read James 2, the passage about how faith without works is dead, and that scripture coloured my whole thinking. I realised that I had been practising my religion but I wasn't living the life and actually faith and life are the same thing, you don't become a different person on a Sunday. If your faith is important to you, then it is part of you, it is who you are.

While we were students, Kim went to Tanzania to work in a mission hospital. I knew that she always had a heart to work overseas. I didn't, but I knew that if I married her, this would be a part of our life. So, I guess I had to bite the bullet and say, 'Yeah, I'll give it a go.' When we met I'd never been out of the country before. We had some friends in Kenya, so Kim took me to visit. I think that she was trying to get me used to the idea of going overseas, but I was petrified before we'd even left the runway. Just the thought of being in an aeroplane made me white knuckled and clammy. Then God's sense of humour kicked in again as someone told me, 'You've got to remember, the pilot wants to get there as much as you do. He's not going to fly the plane unless he's absolutely happy.' Those words gave me the reassurance that I could hand over the flight to the pilot, who also had a family, and wouldn't want to be taking risks.

Once I'd got used to the idea of travelling, Kim persuaded me that we should at least do something in terms of mission work overseas. I was working as a general practitioner at the time, but when we started to apply, it became obvious to me that I would need more than generalist skills. Important issues to do with strategy, planning and taking a longer-term approach were needed. At the time there was a community health course, which was four years full-time training, so I did that with a view to working overseas and got a post in England, working in public health.

At this point, my thoughts of going overseas were still linked with Kenya, and I had visions of myself sitting under the shade of a banyan tree, eating mangoes. Like I said, God had other ideas. We applied to a charity called Tearfund and were offered a placement to go and work for a year, leading a team in a Khmer Rouge camp of 40,000 refugees on the Thai/ Cambodian border. I agreed, very reluctantly. Flying out to a war zone wasn't what I had in mind at all, especially when I heard that the camp was being shelled. I was terrified.

It was surprising how quickly we became used to the dull thud of shells, and the feel of the earth shaking under our feet after an explosion. It wasn't that we ever became blasé about it, but it became the norm. It did test me, because we've all got our limits, but for me, I've just got to be sensible.

I'm not a hero. If I felt my life was at risk, I probably wouldn't do it. Some years later I was asked if I would go to a more remote part of Cambodia, but it was where the Khmer Rouge was still active and where kidnappings were happening. I thought about my family and decided I'd rather not do that.

Our first trip to Cambodia was in 1989, which was some years after the genocide. The camp was well established and well organised. If you just went into an acute refugee situation for a short time you would probably only see the hurt and the destruction. Some missionaries describe a three- to six-month period where they question what they're doing. We certainly questioned helping refugees, particularly the Khmer Rouge who were responsible under Pol Pot for the genocide. Every time I met one, I would ask, 'Why did you work under Pol Pot? Why were you part of the Khmer Rouge?' Then I heard their stories.

The people from this camp had fled from the Vietnamese border, and told me that many had their families killed in blanket bombing by the Americans. Pol Pot and the Khmer Rouge had taken them in as orphans, looked after them and fed them. Their perception of the Khmer Rouge was that they were good for them, and not everywhere in Cambodia was as bad as the areas known as the killing fields. They also had hatred for Westerners and naturally were apprehensive about us going in to help. Their reaction taught me a lot about relationships. Perhaps I've got a bit of Stockholm syndrome, but I realised if you show people that you're not judgemental and you're there to help unreservedly, then relationships can be built. I learned that working overseas isn't about going out with a Western mind-set and doing something, leaving and that's it. It's about relationships, it's about people, it's about doing something that makes a difference, bringing about a change that stays when you go home.

We went with the intention of staying one year and we ended up staying two. I found the Khmers to be lovely people, who were receptive to learning and wanted to go back to their country to do the best for their country. Working with the refugees wasn't just about helping the people, they helped me. They changed my view on life because as a refugee it's all about survival. They don't necessarily think about tomorrow or the day after. They think about what is important in life. When I did the same, I realised for me, the important things were faith, family and friends. It was a realisation that was to colour my whole future.

When Kim and I went out to Cambodia, we both had careers as doctors and we didn't have children. Children came along partly because we realised that family life was important enough for us to try to have children, but if we'd stayed in the UK, we might have just had parallel careers and I don't know what would've happened. All I can say is that experience in Cambodia coloured our family life and how we viewed family life.

The refugees also coloured what I wanted to do in medicine, which was not just about the physical aspects of care, but about more holistic care. I realised that the emotional and spiritual side of care is important too.

When I returned from Cambodia I got a job as a director of public health and later I moved again into palliative care, where I still work. In a sense the attitudes you find in a refugee situation are similar to how people feel when they are in hospice care. When you are working with refugees, yes there are physical needs, but there is also need for hope, purpose and a sense of the future. Palliative care is the same. It isn't just about helping someone with their pain. When a person is coming to the end of their life they are not worried about a dent on the car or that the washing machine has broken down. What's important at that time is family, it's about relationships, it's about thinking that you've done something meaningful with your life, that your life hasn't been wasted. What's important? What gives you fulfilment? I guess, coloured by the refugees I met I've always followed that kind of philosophy, that what I do should be meaningful, and that I shouldn't keep putting off what I want to do because I don't know what is going to happen next year. I'm not saying that I've done anything meaningful, but it's proved to me that there's a fulfilment in doing something that you think is beneficial. In a sense, you could say that the refugees taught me what vocation is.

Since those two years, I've done overseas consultancies in other countries including Rwanda, Iran and the Ukraine, but I've always had an attachment to Cambodia and have continued to work there both with Tearfund and with a charity called Transform Asia. Now we step off the plane and feel very much at home, there are people we know and we are visiting places we've been to in the past.

The work that I do now in Cambodia isn't all medical. It would be very easy for me as a doctor to go out and run clinics then leave. That would help people in the short term, but with my public health background I wanted to take a more strategic approach, because we found that their needs are often more basic than that. In one remote community, they didn't have water handy so we funded a well. In another community the people wanted to be self-sufficient in meat, so we helped to build a chicken coop where they could raise chickens, eat their own meat and sell it. When we went back, the chicken coop had expanded and was making a bit of a profit, which was great to see, because for me it is about developing people and leaving skills, and also about forming friendships and relationships.

If it wasn't for getting involved in Christian ministry and working with refugees, I wouldn't have the family that I have. My wife and I probably wouldn't have the relationship that we have, and I probably wouldn't have ended up where I have in medicine. On one level, my life has all been coincidence, but I don't believe that they are coincidences, because I believe that God plays a part and has had his hand on my life all the way through. The exciting thing is, I don't know where it will lead. If it all stops tomorrow, I'll be happy, but I know that God has got a real sense of humour about the future; I just don't know what it will be.

20 *Listening to God*

Mary Butterwick

Mary Butterwick OBE is founder of the Butterwick
Hospice in Stockton. When her husband died it set
Mary on a course to change the face of palliative care
in the North East of England. Driven by hope for a
better world, and an unwavering faith, against all odds
she succeeded.

John Sentamu writes:

I grew up in a large family, one of thirteen children. We used to have a saying in our house: 'You have two eyes to see, two ears to hear, and one mouth to speak – stop talking and start listening!'

At Bishopthorpe Palace, we ring a large gong every day at midday. It sounds three times, and lasts for about a minute.

During the period the gong sounds, we stop what we are doing – just for a short time – and use the peace and quiet to reflect and pray.

It's important that during our busy lives we take moments like this to stop and refocus on what is important. It's great to have a time we can be close to God – with no phone calls, conversations or pressing work intruding in.

It is easy to get caught up in our own thoughts, dreams and ambitions, but we need to learn to seek God's guidance and trust in him. God has a purpose for our lives. It's important that we see space to listen and then follow – too often we do things in our own strength.

This chapter looks at the story of Mary who listened to God – and set up a hospice in Stockton. Her willingness to follow God's call helped transform palliative care in the North East of England, and touch the lives of countless families going through difficult times.

I only hope that I have her energy, enthusiasm and determination to follow God when I am eighty-eight years old!

✥

I often tell people that their life changes in a moment, and it does. One minute you're merrily sauntering down one road, then all of a sudden the path changes and you find yourself hurtling in another direction. That's how it's been in my life, anyway.

Up until 1979 my life was tootling along happily. My husband John and I had just celebrated thirty-three years of marriage, our four children had left home and married themselves, and I had taken a part-time job at a tea factory.

I thought that everything would keep rolling on as it always had done. Then, with no warning, John took ill and two weeks later he was dead. At first we were told that John had something wrong with a muscle or a nerve behind his eye. I had no idea how serious it was until he fell into a coma. It was only then that doctors told me John had a brain tumour. By that time he couldn't respond and it was too late to say goodbye.

My life changed completely when I lost my husband. There were so many unanswered questions. Why did no one tell me that John was dying? Surely they must have known. Why did I not see it myself? Had John known and not told me? Why were we robbed of our last farewell? Why did we not have time to say, I love you? Why was John allowed to fall three times in the hospital? Why was there no compassion from the staff? Why did a ward sister tell me to go home and forget him because I could do nothing for him any more? Maybe that nurse cared for John physically and medically, but why couldn't she have been more careful with her words?

In those days people didn't talk about cancer. It was referred to as the dirty big C and some people even thought it was catching. I wanted to know more. I wanted to know how people were coping with this because I wasn't coping. The doctors were medically taking care of people, but what about the emotional pain, who was helping with that?

In my frustration and grief I questioned God. Why John? Why did he die this way? Where is the care, where is the love? Where is God in all of this mess? There was so much I wanted to know – about death, dying and the afterlife. Of course I didn't always find the answers I was seeking. Sometimes I only found more questions, but in my searching I opened up a conversation with God. I admitted to God that I didn't have it all together, that I had serious deep wounds that I didn't know how to heal. Jesus said, 'Come to me, all of you who are tired and have heavy loads, and I will give you rest.' Well, I felt heavy-laden, and here I was crying out for his help.

Bereavement can be a very self-pitying time. I thought no one could feel the grief I felt or that my life would ever be the same again. Life wasn't the same again, but I did learn in time to live a new life, and found that life could be good again. Finding myself with more time on my hands, I volunteered with a community group for people with disabilities. Being part of that group stopped me focusing on myself and my own pain. Of course, the pain didn't go away completely, but the group gave me a diversion and I began to turn a corner in my grief. In taking my mind off my problems I was helping myself and others, as well as the organisation I was volunteering for, so it was a three-way win.

In time, as I began to mix with other people again, I did begin to forgive some of the medical staff for the way they treated John and I during his illness but I couldn't forget the unnecessary pain caused by the neglect I'd felt. There had to be a better way to help families facing a similar situation, I just didn't know what it was. Initially I felt hopeless, but then I realised that whenever I felt that there was nothing I could do, of course there was – I could pray.

Each lunch time when I got home from the tea factory I would sit at the table with my cup of coffee, read a passage from the Bible, and ask God to open my heart and allow me to take whatever I needed from the reading. I suppose, although I wasn't aware of it at the time, I was inviting the Holy Spirit to guide me.

One day after my daily prayer time I felt an urge to write. I often found writing therapeutic, a way to get my thoughts together and make sense of the noise in my head. This day I found myself writing about a house where cancer patients and their families could come and talk through their anxieties and fears. I saw it all, from the glowing fireplace to the pictures on the walls. I could even smell the fresh flowers on the table and feel the thick-piled carpet underfoot. It was an uplifting place, where people could visit for a day, or even half a day. They would eat wholesome, home-made food, having a bit of what they fancied when they fancied it. If they wanted to read they could read; if they wanted to chat they could chat; if they wanted to play dominoes let them play dominoes. Care and companionship were the only rules of this house. That said, if this home was going to offer care and support for the terminally ill, then I supposed it would need a doctor, or at least a nurse. Someone who knew what they were doing in terms of medicine. Yet, for every medic, it would need at least twenty other people – caring people who could help with other things, important things that can so easily get overlooked in times of ill health, like help with finances, help with cleaning and shopping, and arranging days out. For all those whom the hospital had dismissed as beyond help, it would restore hope, celebrate life and, even if it couldn't heal the body, it would do its best to heal the heart and soul.

The idea sounded wonderful, but who would listen to me? I wasn't a wealthy or an educated woman. I realised that no one would take any notice of a 54-year-old grieving widow, so for a long time I only shared my dream with a couple of friends. I asked them to pray about it and I did too, but God helps those who help themselves, and I knew that if this was to happen then I'd have to take some kind of action. Before I could ask anyone else to help I'd have to put my money where my mouth was, and the only money I had was in my home.

Now, there are lots of ways we can help to make other people's lives better and I'm not advocating that anyone sell their house as I did. At the time I couldn't see any other way. I was almost at retiring age, who would've listened to me? If I wanted people to believe in change then I had to be able to say 'I've done this, now will you help me to do that?' Even after I sold my house I couldn't have moved forward if it hadn't been for other people helping me.

I soon discovered God's path is never smooth. I found the ideal property for a day care centre, but it was under offer and three contracts had to fall through on it before my offer was finally accepted. When I did secure the sale, the renovations needed were so extensive that I had to sleep on any spare sofa I could find until the work was complete. Yet, despite the obstacles it was like a miracle the way it all started to come together.

When we opened Butterwick House in 1984 it was the first day care centre in the North East for people with terminal illness and their families. We ran like that for five years, but more and more people started to ask me about beds, somewhere for people to go at the end of their life, where they could die, pain-free and with dignity. Although people didn't use the word, they were asking for a hospice. I totted up the costs involved and it seemed impossible, but I'd felt that before about the day care centre. I couldn't say if the idea would succeed or fail. All I knew was that if it was to succeed it would need the backing of the community, so I decided to hold an open meeting to see how strong the feeling for a hospice really was.

If there was any doubt before the meeting, there was none after it. The hall was packed with people standing in the aisles. I stood at the front and spoke about why I believed Teesside needed a hospice and what I thought would be involved in making that happen. Then I invited questions from the floor. My heart flipped when a district nurse stood up first, because in the early days I'd faced so much opposition from medical staff who felt that I was meddling in areas that I knew nothing about. 'I don't know how it can be done, but I agree we do need this palliative care,' she said. To my amazement everyone clapped as a chorus of agreement ran through the crowd. It was clear that the people of Teesside wanted a hospice and they were going to support the Butterwick Trust in providing one. Exactly how any of it would happen was a question for another day, but I trusted in God that it would.

Today Butterwick Hospice Care helps up to 200 patients and their families each day, with two dedicated adult hospice units and a children's unit.

I never imagined any of this when I set out. I couldn't have imagined how it would grow. The staff and the patients at the hospice are just part of the story. Now there are people who climb mountains, trek through jungles and bungee jump off Middlesbrough's Transporter Bridge, all to raise money for the hospice. It is amazing to think how far we've come, but, like many things in life, it was achieved through stepping stones. If your heart is in it you've just got to do what you can, step out in faith and trust there will be another stone to catch you.

So many people over the years have said to me, 'It's outrageous that you have to raise all this money,' but it's not. We could do with a little bit more help, of course we could. It would've made everybody's job a bit easier if we got it all paid, but that wouldn't have been the same thing – it wouldn't then be about all the volunteers and everything they give, which can't be paid for. A hospice is about community because without the community putting its share into it, it wouldn't be any different to any other health service.

Even after all these years I still hear people talk about hospices as if they are simply a place where people go to die. It all sounds incredibly morbid. Death is a natural part of life and it is a shame that we have to keep running from it to the point where fear stops us enjoying the life we have. Many have died at Butterwick Hospice and, no doubt, many more will. There have been many tears but there is also much laughter, because everyone who dies at the hospice has also lived at the hospice and I hope that the care provided allows them to enjoy the life they have.

For a long time I've known that the hospice would run along just fine without me, but at eighty-eight years old I still volunteer when I can, because I find that whatever I give in this way I get back tenfold.

The self-pity I felt in grief can happen to a lot of people, be that through unemployment, divorce or whatever. We all need to feel a sense of belonging and value. If you can find a job where your heart is then you're very fortunate, but if it's just to pay the groceries at the end of the week, volunteering can give you that sense of contribution. And there are so many ways to volunteer today – whatever you are interested in you'll find some encouragement if you're willing to give some time.

Whatever some people might say, it's not about giving something for nothing. If you don't receive anything then very soon you won't give anything. You've got to get something out of it yourself. The patients at the hospice give me something much more valuable than money can buy. We're helping and supporting each other and that's how life should be.

DARTON · LONGMAN + TODD

Darton, Longman and Todd is as an internationally-respected publisher of brave, ground-breaking and independent books on matters of heart, mind and soul that meet the needs and interests of ordinary people.

Our books are written by, and for, people of all faiths and none. We believe that spirituality and faith are important to all people, of all backgrounds, and that the wisdom of any one culture or tradition can inform and nourish another.

We also publish the Jerusalem Bible, and its revised and updated successor, the New Jerusalem Bible – one of the most clear, accurate and distinguished modern English translations of the Bible.

For more information on DLT, and to buy our books, please visit our website
www.dltbooks.com
or visit your local bookshop. You can stay up to date with our activities by following us on Twitter @dlt_books

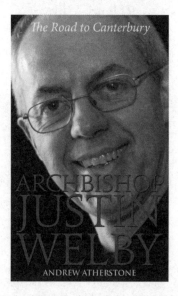

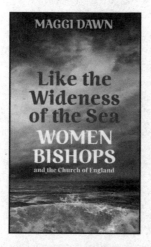